REASONS
I

REASONS I

Sects and Cults with Non-Christian Roots

Bill Evenhouse

Cover: Dean Heetderks

Bible Way

Grand Rapids, Michigan

Library of Congress Cataloging in Publication Data

Evenhouse, Bill, 1939–
   Reasons I, sects and cults with non-Christian roots.

   Bibliography: p.
   1. Cults. 2. Apologetics—20th century.
I. Title. II. Title: Sects and cults with non-Christian roots.
BP603.E94   291   81-10117
ISBN 9-933140-23-1   AACR2

Always be prepared to give an answer to everyone who asks you to give the reason for the hope that you have. But do this with gentleness and respect. . . .
1 Peter 3:15–16 (NIV)

Contents

Preface

This is the first in a series of four books in the course entitled Reasons. *That title is borrowed from Peter's injunction to "Always be prepared. . . to give the reason for the hope that you have." It's a course that's intended to help Reformed Christians give reasons for their faith when conversing with people who hold another faith.*

Reasons *is offered as part of the BIBLE WAY curriculum for young adults. That doesn't mean that this book and course won't be profitable for you if you don't think of yourself as falling in that rather vague category.* Reasons *is usable by a variety of age groups, from mature high school seniors to the oldest adults. All Christians of all ages should learn to give reasons for what they believe.*

Still, sects and cults, other faiths, and different understandings of the Christian faith are a particular concern for young people in their very late teens and early twenties. Those are often unsettled years when young men and women are leaving home communities and finding their own niche in life. The instability that comes with such a basic life change can make otherwise well-adjusted people peculiarly vulnerable to the lure of some offbeat religious groups and strange new ideas.

This book will introduce you to eight sects and cults with non-Christian roots. It's intended to prepare you, as a Christian, to understand the teachings and attractions of these groups and to speak to their adherents.

The author of this book is Mr. William Evenhouse. A native of Grand Rapids, Michigan, Mr. Evenhouse graduated from Calvin College and the University of Michigan (M.A. in Creative Writing). After teaching in the United States for several years and doing further graduate work in linguistics, he went to Nigeria for the Christian Reformed Board of World Missions and worked there from 1965 to 1980 as a teacher and linguist. He is presently employed in the Curriculum Department for Christian Schools International.

Background research for this book required an expert's in-depth knowledge and perception. These were provided by Dr. J. William Smit, professor of sociology at Calvin College. A graduate of that institution and of the University of Michigan, Dr. Smit has a special interest in the sociology of religion.

The session guides in this book were prepared by the Education Department staff.

Harvey A. Smit
Director of Education

MAKING AN APOLOGY

Reasons is a course in apologetics. That's a field of theological study and not—as the word seems to suggest—a way of saying you're sorry.

The word *apologetics* comes from ancient Athens. When an Athenian citizen was charged with some crime or illegal action, he had the right to defend his actions publicly before his fellow citizens. That defense was called an apology.

The Bible uses this same word several times. In Acts 19, for instance, when the people of Ephesus were upset by Paul's preaching, Alexander, a local believer, stood up and tried to make a defense or apology for Paul (v. 33). Also, the apostle Peter warns Christians spread through Asia Minor and facing imminent persecution: "Always be prepared to make a defense [apology] to anyone who calls you to account for the hope that is in you..." (1 Pet. 3:15 RSV).

Apologetics then is the study of how Christians may best defend their faith. *Reasons* is a course designed to help you make such apologies.

According to the Peter's clear injunction, defending the faith is something each of us should be prepared to do. Christian philosophers often make such a defense in writing against non-Christian or anti-Christian thinkers. In the same way ordinary believers should be prepared to defend the faith while conversing with non-Christian people across the backyard fence or at the office party.

Doing apology clearly does *not* mean apologizing for Christ or making excuses for what you believe or how you act. Instead it means you should be ready to say what you believe and explain why you believe as you do whenever you are challenged to do so. If a convinced Baptist asks why you were baptized as an infant, if friends inquire why you won't join them for a Sunday morning golf game, if Jehovah's Witnesses come to your door and want to know why you won't visit their Kingdom Hall, or if a fellow worker asks why you refuse to take any moral shortcuts—you should be able to give reasons, faith reasons, why you act as you do. That kind of defense is one of the obligations of the Christian faith.

Making such apologies is important partly for your own sake (How can anyone be confident in a faith that can't be defended or reasonably explained?) and partly for the sake of others (How else can anyone see the attraction of the gospel except as it immediately relates to a believer's life?). So for both your neighbor's good and your own, being prepared to give reasons for your faith is a valuable exercise.

This textbook, *Reasons I,* is intended to help prepare you to make apology to members of various sects and cults with non-Christian roots. What do we mean by sects and cults?

Generally a religious group is called a cult if it makes a definite break with the traditional religion of the society. Cults usually claim some special revelation from God by which they reinterpret or add to the generally accepted religious writings (Bible, Koran, etc.). Cults also are usually built around a strong leader who insists on strict discipline and has absolute authority over his or her followers. Cults, if they last long enough, may become a new religion. The Moonies are an example of a cult.

A sect, on the other hand, is a small religious group that has broken with some traditional religious system or denomination but has not done so radically. A sect is usually trying to get back to the original true faith, not found a radically new faith. It still accepts the religious writings of the main group as authoritative. Sects tend more toward lay leadership and permit more individualism than cults do. Hare Krishna is an example of a Hindu sect.

The line between sects and cults isn't absolute, but it's still important. Because of the different quality of leadership and kind of authority recognized, one generally deals differently with disciples of a cult and members of a sect.

This book contains eight challenges, each of which treats a specific sect or cult. These challenges try to give you not only some basic information about this religious group but also the flavor of these people's faith—why they believe and act as they do and why they are able to attract others into their group. The challenge is finally intended, as the name implies, to invite you to respond, to summon you to consider what you would say or do if you happened to meet such a person.

We're asking you, together with others who are taking this course, to consider that challenge and how you might best respond. A group discussion should help you recognize the strengths and weaknesses of your own church's position, how prepared or unprepared you are to make such an apology, and what the best approach might be.

After the group discussion (or sometime during it), we've suggested that your teacher or discussion leader hand out the author's response to the challenge. The approach the author takes is not the one, authoritative answer—the only good way to respond. You may disagree with it. You may have already reached some other conclusion. Still each response will give you, for future reference, the thoughtful ideas of someone who has studied this group with care. An envelope has been provided on the back cover of this book for storing the author's responses.

It's our earnest hope that this course will not only strengthen your understanding of your own faith, but also begin to equip you to deal confidently and positively with believers of various sects and cults. It's with that hope that we offer this book for your study.

Harvey A. Smit
Director of Education

The Rev. Sun Myung Moon

THE UNIFICATION CHURCH

The Holy Spirit Association
for the Unification of World Christianity

Founding: Sun Myung Moon (1902–), once a member of the Presbyterian Church in Korea, founded the Unification Church in 1954. After the Korean War, Moon's following grew rapidly in Korea and spread to Japan.

In 1972 Moon had a "divine revelation" telling him to emigrate to the United States. Today, after convincing thousands of Americans to give him their money and join his church, the wealthy Moon has gone into semiretirement: although he remains the spiritual head of the church, Mose Durst has taken over as president of the Unification Church in America.

Following: The Unification Church claims 30,000 adherents in the United States, one million worldwide. Most "Moonies" live in Korea, Japan, North America, and Europe.

Faith: *God is a single being who unites in himself all the opposites, male and female, good and evil, and so on.
*If Adam and Eve had not fallen into sin but been perfected, they, as the true parents, would have formed a trinity with God.
*Humanity fell spiritually when Eve had sexual intercourse with Lucifer (Satan).

*Jesus, the second Adam, was unable to save humanity physically because Satan made him impotent. However, he did save humanity spiritually through his death on the cross.
*Jesus did not rise from the dead; he only appeared as a spirit being.
*The Lord of the Second Advent is the messiah (already) born in Korea (2,000 years after Christ). He will accomplish physical salvation.

Monday, June 1

The tricky part would be how to keep Mother from getting upset. Sandy hesitated before depositing the coins. She looked across the busy room toward Rodney's table. Grace saw her and made a funny face while hunching her shoulders up almost to her ears. Sandy had to laugh.

She deposited the coins, waited for the operator, then gave her the home number and the credit card number. Benny answered the phone. That was good. The folks were at a church meeting. That made it easier.

"Just tell them not to worry," she said. "I'll be home by Wednesday for sure. The car broke down on the freeway near Concord, and I barely got it to the garage. The man said he'll have it ready over the weekend."

"Where are you staying?" Benny's voice sounded distant; he was probably watching TV while talking to her.

"That's all set. I met these really nice kids, and they just sort of put me up."

"Are they weird?"

"Don't be dopey." Sandy laughed. "No, they're really nice. As nice as I've ever known. They're even kinda serious. They're going up to a sort of farm they have for the weekend, and I'm going along. When I get back, the car'll be ready and I'll come home."

"Don't be late for school."

"Not to worry. Registration is Friday. I can make it in two days. Expect me Wednesday. Okay?"

"Okay."

She could tell Benny was already somewhere else. She hung up the phone and walked back to Grace and Rodney. "All set," she said.

By noon her feet were hurting and her back was tired, but she was surprised to find she really didn't care. She'd never met this kind of a bunch before. They never seemed to run out of love. Or energy. Two lectures and discussions, and now lunch and another lecture, and then a volleyball game. The lunch had better be pure sugar.

One U.C. official told me, "If someone's lonely, we talk to them. There are a lot of lonely people walking around."

Berkeley Rice, "Honor Thy Father," *Psychology Today,* January 1976

"Moonie" is a term outsiders have used to designate followers of the Rev. Sun Myung Moon. Many members of the Unification Church accept the term themselves.

"The Moonies Cross Wits with Cult-Watching Critics," *Christianity Today,* July 20, 1979

"Coming?" Ruthie, one of the regular members, put her arm around Sandy's shoulders. "Tired, huh? But that'll go away. The more you understand what we're doing for the world, and what we *will* do, the less you think about being tired, or hungry, or anything else like that. It becomes so unimportant."

Through lunchtime that didn't make much sense, but by 3:00, in the middle of the volleyball game, she began to get the idea. Ruthie, who had been at her side all day helping explain some of the harder things in the lectures, was in charge of her team. She was everywhere, clapping all of them on the back and shouting encouragement. "Love and win!" she chanted, "Love and win!" Then they were in the middle of the game, and Sandy had joined the chant. "Love and win," she murmured, over and over, playing hard but not really caring who won at all.

It's the love I feel, she thought. It keeps me going. She repeated the phrase while watching the excited faces surrounding her. The shouts, the noise. She thought of a circus when she was small, repeated again "Love and win," and dove for the ball as it came her way. Tripping over her own feet, she stumbled to the sideline and sprawled on the grass.

Suddenly there were arms around her again and faces.

"Are you okay?"

"Gotta get your breath!"

"Sit up. Hey, you're crying!"

And she was, but she didn't care at all. They were literally tears of joy. She threw her arms back, the tiredness gone, and sobbed, "I just realized I love you guys. All of you! I really do!"

Tuesday, September 7
Napa Valley

Dear Mom and Dad,

By the time you get this you'll probably have already worried yourselves sick—but please stop now 'cause I'm all right. I would have called to tell you I decided to stay on for another week, but there aren't any phones in the area. In fact, the last phone I saw was the one I used to call Benny.

Since then lots of things have happened. I went to the retreat with Grace and Rodney (who you don't know, but I'm sure you'd like—they're great kids). The first retreat was only two days and, even though I didn't understand much of it at all, I had a lot of fun. Everybody there was really sweet and friendly. They told me that if I really wanted to understand what it was all about I could stay on for a seven-day workshop.

I felt I shouldn't, knowing I'd miss the registration for the fall term, but everybody here cared so much. And what they said made sense: *what's more important— getting another semester of college in or really finding out who I am and what's really worthwhile in life anyway?*

So I've stayed. After all, if I decide to leave, it's only a semester gone. More than half of the new kids did leave—but they were kind of distant from the rest anyway.

The workshop ends Saturday, but another one starts right after it, and some of us are staying on. I've already decided to stay. There's so much about the world I never really realized, and so much I have to try to grasp. I wish Benny were here—but he'd probably just laugh at how serious we are. I'm studying the *Divine Principle* and really trying to decide just why I want to find out about the Unification Church. It's not like our church at home, that much I know. In the next workshop I've been told we'll learn how to witness and work for the church. I remember how the word *witness* used to sound stupid to me, but here it makes good sense.

If you want to send me some of my savings you can, but you don't need to; everybody here works for the church and in turn we get what we need.

Don't worry—I haven't run away. I'm fine and I'll write again.

All my love,

Sandy

Most Moonies seem genuinely happy in their service to Moon and the Church. In exchange for their labor, devotion and commitment, the Church has given them a home, a family, and a purpose. Critics may call that exploitation or slavery, but the Moonies consider it a bargain.

Berkeley Rice, "Honor Thy Father," *Psychology Today,* January 1976

Once the second workshop starts, then that's it. It's really intense. . . .

Tom Gillespie (after two years as an active U.C. member), "To the Moon and Back," an interview in *Psychiatric Nursing,* March–April 1980

Monday, October 18

The cafe was quiet and dark, and she didn't recognize her father's business partner until he turned toward her. He was reaching for his wallet, and his hand stopped halfway. In his other hand he held the flowers she'd just given him.

"Sandy!" he said. "So you're a Moonie!"

Sandy smiled, "You must've known that, Mr. Howard. You work with Dad and, besides, you're an elder in our church." For a moment she wondered if he'd been sent to get her. But he fished his wallet out and extracted a five dollar bill and handed it to her.

"Steep for the flowers," he said. "Do you really believe it?"

"Believe what?"

"This Rev. Moon, claiming to be God or whatever."

She smiled again. You could depend on it—they would always have it wrong. The instructors had told her so, and it had been true every time.

"He doesn't claim that at all. Just teaches us how to receive and give love the way the world needs it."

"By wearing those old clothes?"

For a moment she was tempted to anger, but she prayed a short mind-prayer to her true Father, and immediately she saw he'd meant nothing by the remark.

"I always wore nice clothes and had nice things before," she said slowly. "And I never really knew how alone and lost I was until I met Grace and Rodney and Ruthie and the rest."

"Who are they? Other Moonies?"

She knew she shouldn't say it; she knew it would get back home and hurt those she never wanted to hurt at all, but another part of her remembered the discussion the night before. "They'll say you've rejected them," Beth had told them as they watched her intently. "But it's they who don't want the truth. It's they who've joined forces with Satan. And it's you who have to do all in your power to save them!"

"They're my family, Mr. Howard," she said, "my new family." She noticed Ruthie motioning to her from the door. "I have to go now," she said.

FOR FURTHER READING

Edwards, Christopher. *Crazy for God*. Englewood Cliffs, N.J.: Prentice Hall, 1979.

According to *Insight* magazine (April 1981), this book tells Edwards's story of "seven nightmare months in which he was held captive and changed from a stubbornly independent college graduate into a totally submissive disciple of Moon. . . . What happened to Chris Edwards could happen to anyone. . . . The book also answers questions about what cults do, what it's like to live in one. . . ."

Enroth, Ronald. *Youth, Brainwashing, and the Extremist Cults*. Grand Rapids, Mich.: Zondervan Corporation, 1977.

Christian sociologist looks at several cults accused of brainwashing.

Schipper, Earl. *Cults in North America*. Grand Rapids, Mich.: Christian Schools International, 1980.

Part of the Biblical Perspective series used in many Christian schools. Covers five major cults.

Sontag, Frederick. *Sun Myung Moon and the Unification Church*. Nashville, Tenn.: Abingdon Press, 1977.

An unbiased view of the Unification Church based on interviews of Moon, Moonies, and anti-Moonies. Includes a section on what the movement can teach us.

CASSETTE TAPES

Martin, Walter. *The Truth about Rev. Sun Myung Moon*. C-55. Available from the Christian Research Institute, Box 500, San Juan Capistrano, California 92693. Write for brochure and current prices.

Unification Church Promotion

SESSION GUIDE

CHALLENGE 1   THE UNIFICATION CHURCH

A. Personal notes/questions on Challenge 1

B. The Moonie challenge

    1. Check out the beliefs of the Moonies. They claim to be Christians. Are they?

    2. What attracted Sandy to the Unification Church? Was it the beliefs of the church or something else? Explain.

    3. Review the process of how Sandy became a Moonie. Would you say Sandy had been brainwashed—or are Moonie tactics similar to those used by any evangelical group to win converts? Explain.

    4. Do you think it possible that you or your friends could be attracted to the Moonies—or does the Unification Church appeal mainly to unstable individuals with nonreligious, problem-filled backgrounds? Explain.

C. Our response

"If you were Mr. Howard, what would you say to Sandy? What would you do?"

Consider the advantages and disadvantages of the following alternatives. Then pick the one(s) you would use.

1. Let Sandy go. Say nothing to anyone. There's nothing you can do to help. It's not your responsibility anyway.

2. Invite Sandy to sit down, have a Coke, and tell you everything that's happened to her. Just listen.

3. Listen to Sandy's story (as above), but then attempt to convince her, biblically, that the Unification Church is wrong. Set a time for talking more about this.

4. Listen to Sandy now. Set a time for talking to her later. At that time try to help Sandy recognize that her social and spiritual needs are now being met by the Moonies, but that the church can meet these same needs—and that the church family is ready and willing to help.

5. Let Sandy go, but talk to her parents and persuade them to arrange another meeting with her, perhaps using Benny as bait. If Sandy takes the bait, seize her, keep her in isolation with a professional deprogrammer until she recognizes the truth and renounces the Moonies.

6. Let Sandy go, but talk to her parents and encourage them to wait (and pray) until Sandy reaches out to them in some way. Then welcome her, accept her, avoid angry confrontations, change as necessary to meet her deepest needs. Hope that a solid Christian home and church will eventually meet Sandy's needs and return her to the faith.

7. Drag Sandy along with you to her parents' home where she belongs. Help the parents attempt to talk some sense into her. Keep her at home until she's ready to go back to college.

8. Other?

Maharishi Mahesh Yogi

TRANSCENDENTAL MEDITATION

Founding: Transcendental Meditation (TM) was founded by Maharishi Mahesh Yogi. The Maharishi, born in India in 1918, became a disciple of the Hindu Guru Dev in 1940. Following the guru's instructions, the Maharishi went into isolation in the Himalayan Mountains to develop a system of meditation for the common person. In 1959 he brought that system, TM, to California and presented it not as Hindu meditation, but as a "nonreligious" technique.

Following: In 1977 the cult claimed about a million meditators in North America. Transcendental Meditation is also being taught in many public high schools, a few junior high schools, and over three hundred colleges, mostly at government expense.

Faith:
*God is the impersonal "Creative Intelligence" which finds happiness in creating and includes everything that exists.
*Human beings go through an endless cycle of reincarnations.
*Happiness is attained by diving within ourselves to discover our creative intelligence, thus ridding ourselves of ignorance of who we are. This discovery is "bliss consciousness."
*"Bliss consciousness" is only attained through the seven steps of Transcendental Meditation.
*"Bliss consciousness" comes not by intellectual study but by meditating on a private mantra, a secret, pleasant-sounding, meaningless word assigned by a TM instructor.
*Transcendental Meditation is a secular "science," not a religion.

Four high school students (Mike, Patricia, Vera, and Jerry), in charge of a Christian fellowship group at school, have just begun a meeting.

Mike: Okay, we'd better get started. I've got to leave in twenty minutes. Who's in charge of this meeting?

Patricia: Vera should be. We'll elect new officers this afternoon, but till then she's still president from last year.

Mike: Fair enough, but let's get started.

Vera: We don't need a treasurer's report: I know we have zero assets and zero debts. So there's only one thing to decide, but it's big.

Patricia: What's that?

Vera: Some activity or project to interest old members and attract new ones. The Bible study groups have dropped in attendance. The only things that really drew kids were the movie and the cookout. We need something that will get them here week in and week out.

Mike: Try a different rock band every Wednesday as a substitute for doctrine class.

Patricia: C'mon, get serious. We need something solid.

Mike: Face it, we can't come up with something the kids want that they don't already have.

Jerry: What about peace of mind?

Mike: What've you got in mind now, Jerry, the latest drug?

Jerry: Look, forget that, will you? Actually, I don't want to push anything on you guys. But if you're looking for something the whole group'll use and really want, I've got the answer.

Vera: Go ahead. Nobody else is coming up with anything.

Jerry: Let me ask a couple questions first. Everybody you know is too busy, right?

Patricia: That's life.

Jerry: So if anyone really has a way to help people

"get it all together," everyone's gonna want it, right?

Mike: Makes sense.

Jerry: Well, somebody named Maharishi Mahesh Yogi has a way. It's something that can help all of us. And if we can get our fellowship group to offer it to the school, I guarantee the kids will love it.

Vera: "Yogi" sounds oriental or something. How do you fit it in with a bunch of Christian kids?

Jerry: That's what's so neat about it. For a long time people have thought that meditation and yoga were just for the Hindu religion and not for the West at all. But the Maharishi has taken the essence of the Hindu wisdom and removed all the religion from it. He's reduced it to a techique that can fit any religion. But it gives people who use it the benefits that go along with a truly expanded mind.

Patricia: For instance?

Jerry: Well, drugs for one thing. All sorts of tests have proved that people who were on drugs cut down or stopped when they started practicing Transcendental Meditation. TM users have more energy at work and get more enjoyment out of life in general. They even need less sleep. Twenty minutes of meditation is worth about six hours of sleep.

Mike: You're kidding.

Jerry: I'm not! Your pulse rate goes down and your breathing deepens. Your mind enters a truly relaxed state different from either sleeping or dreaming. And when you've finished, you're really renewed, ready to go out and get something done.

Vera: You sound awfully enthusiastic. Who did you learn all this stuff from?

Jerry: It's an ancient knowledge, passed down over the centuries, usually by a single master to

The Maharishi insists that TM theory be kept separate from various philosophies or metaphysical systems . . . because they will usually muddle one's understanding of the TM process.

Peter Russell, *The TM Technique,* p. 17

The TM process is one of allowing the stronger levels of mental activity to reduce, permitting the subtler underlying levels to enter consciousness.

Peter Russell, *The TM Technique,* p. 24

29

his disciple. But the Maharishi changed all that. He has personally trained hundreds, maybe thousands of instructors in the art of teaching these techniques of meditation. Even though the techniques are simple, little mistakes can creep in and make the results less effective. So you need instructors.

Mike: For the next ten years?

Jerry: Nothing like that. About four to six hours in all and after that only to check how you are doing occasionally. It's no big thing—but it has big results.

Vera: What happens during those hours of instruction?

Jerry: Before you start you attend some lectures to tell you what it's all about. Then, if you want to go further, you pay a fee.

Patricia: There had to be a catch!

Jerry: Hold on a minute. There are special rates for students, and besides the whole fee is no more than you pay for a weekend's skiing.

Mike: Okay, what then?

Jerry: You get together this sort of offering and go with your instructor—alone—into a quiet, dark room lit with candles. The instructor chants a song called the *puja*. It's all in Sanskrit and just sets the mood. After that you receive your mantra. That's a special word, chosen especially to suit you, to help you meditate. Then you learn to do a period of meditation which lasts about twenty minutes. During this meditation time, you relax and focus on your secret mantra. Do that twice a day and that's all there's to it.

Vera: That's forty minutes a day. Who'll want to give up that much time?

Jerry: Most people who try it. In the fifties, when Maharishi arrived in California from India, he worked for years to get just a few people interested—a pretty predictable thing considering that most Westerners are skeptical about Eastern mysticism. But in the sixties everything changed. People began to realize he wasn't pushing a new religion—just a technique all people could use to improve the quality of their lives. The movement really caught on. People realized that they could get to a level of experience beyond just tasting, or smelling, or feeling—that they could really get at the essence of how they fit into their world.

Mike: Sounds spaced out.

Jerry: But it's really just the opposite. Drugs take you further and further from the real world. Transcendental Meditation brings you more and more into real harmony with it. Your ability to cope improves. It's just the opposite with drugs. The deeper you get into them, the less you can cope.

Mike: You should know.

Jerry: Lay off; I haven't touched any of that stuff for months. The point is that public schools in a state like Illinois, for example, are starting classes in TM as a regular part of instruction—because they see how much it helps.

Vera: But how can public schools have religion classes in their schools?

Jerry: You forget, this isn't a religion. Seymour Migdal, the dean of the faculty at Maharishi University says: "It doesn't require faith and it doesn't require worship. It's just a helpful technique."

Patricia: So they have a university too?

Jerry: They sure do. And they are willing to send instructors to our school if we have an interest in it. That's why I'm taking your time with this. I think we ought to sponsor it so that the school knows we want it. What better group than ours to push for a really good self-improvement program?

If you think *that you are in the state then you can be pretty sure that you are not, for it lies beyond thought.*

Peter Russell, *The TM Technique*, p. 90

Guru in the glory of Brahma, guru in the glory of Vishnu, guru in the glory of the great Lord Shiva, guru in the glory of personified transcendental fullness of Brahman, to him Shri Guru Dev, adorned with glory, I bow down.

From the *puja*

*The Seven Goals of
TM's World Plan*

1. *To develop the full potential of
the individual*
2. *To improve governmental
achievements*
3. *To realize the highest idea of
education*
4. *To eliminate the age-old problem
of crime and all behavior that
brings unhappiness to the family
of man*
5. *To maximize the intelligent use
of the environment*
6. *To bring fulfillment to the
economic aspirations of
individuals and society*
7. *To achieve the spiritual goals of
mankind in this generation.*

Robert Oates, *Celebrating the Dawn*

Mike: Do you have any real proof this thing works?

Jerry: I think I do. I've been practicing TM for several weeks now. You guys know the sorts of problems I've been dealing with. And it's mostly due to you that they haven't been worse. But in the weeks I've been doing TM there's been a change. Haven't you noticed?

Patricia: Well, I wasn't going to say it, but I *had* been wondering. You *have* seemed a bit easier to take.

Jerry: Check around: I think more people have noticed. And it'll continue. There's tremendous room for self-realization in TM. If you wanted to hear more, I could arrange for some instructors to come and lecture to our fellowship group.

Vera: The main thing is what to say to the group this afternoon. Our time is about up.

Patricia: Why not let Jerry present it to them like he did to us?

Mike: No objection from me.

Vera: Okay. But, Jerry, try to leave time for the elections, okay?

Patricia: For safety's sake, let's cast our votes before he starts to speak!

FOR FURTHER READING

Gerberding, Keith. *How to Respond to Transcendental Meditation.* St. Louis: Concordia, 1977.

A booklet that includes chapters on meditation in the Christian perspective and Christian witnessing to TM advocates.

Haddon, David and Hamilton, Vail. *TM Wants You—Christian Response to Transcendental Meditation.* Grand Rapids, Mich.: Baker Book House, 1976.

Lewis, Gordon. *What Everyone Should Know About Transcendental Meditation.* Glendale, Calif.: Gospel Light Publications, 1975.

Miller, Calvin. *Transcendental Hesitation—A Biblical Appraisal of TM and Eastern Mysticism.* Grand Rapids, Mich.: Zondervan Corporation, 1977.

Shah, Douglas. *The Meditators*, Plainfield, N.J.: Logos, 1975.

    Shah points out the dangers of TM and discusses the art of Christian meditation.

CASSETTE TAPES

Martin, Walter. *Is Transcendental Meditation for You?* C-39. Available from Christian Research Institute, Box 500, San Juan Capistrano, California 92693. Write for current prices and brochure.

Meditation before Making Music

SESSION GUIDE

CHALLENGE 2   TRANSCENDENTAL MEDITATION

A. Personal notes/questions on Challenge 2

B. Challenge and response

If you were a member of this Christian fellowship group, would you be for or against Jerry's proposal? Why?

Discuss this question in small groups, trying to agree on an answer. In your discussion refer as much as possible to specific material in Challenge 2. You might also check Genesis 24:63, Psalm 119:97–99, John 14:6, Philippians 4:8, 1 Thessalonians 5:17, James 2:14–17, and Q & A 1 of the Heidelberg Catechism.

In the space below, list the main reasons for your group's decision:

No, Because they will forget about God. You will get in inveld with TM and will never read the Bible or prey to him.

C. Questions for additional discussion

    1. What positive things can Christians learn from TM?

    2. How can we best help a person like Jerry who insists that TM has a legitimate place in a Christian's life?

    3. Do you have any additional questions of your own?

World-Famous Baha'i House of Worship, Wilmette, Illinois

BAHA'I—THE CHILDREN OF LIGHT

Founding: Baha'i originated in 1844 when Mirza Ali Muhammad took the name Bab (the Gate) and claimed he was the forerunner of a great world teacher—a teacher who would unite all people and bring peace to the world. Muslim officials, alarmed by the Bab's popularity, had him arrested and executed in 1850. But in 1863 Mirza Husayn Ali, one of the Bab's disciples, claimed that *he* was the promised teacher and took the name Bahaullah (the Glory of God). Before he died in 1892, Bahaullah had organized Bab's followers into a new religion: Baha'i (pronounced ba-HA-ee).

Following: In North America an estimated 100,000 members are organized into some 879 Baha'i assemblies. Worldwide over two million members are organized into 72,000 Baha'i centers and communities and 119 national spiritual assemblies.

Faith: *God is one, religion is one, and humanity is one.
*God is unknowable in his essence but has made his name known in each age by divine revelators—including Krishna, Moses, Zoroaster, Gautama Buddha, Jesus Christ, Muhammad, the Bab, and Bahaullah. The followers of all religions should now turn to the new prophet, Bahaullah, for spiritual guidance and pure teachings.
*There should be:
—equality of men and women.
—elimination of all kinds of prejudice.

—abolition of extremes of wealth and poverty.
—universal compulsory education.
—a universal auxiliary language.
—universal peace upheld by a world government.
—glorification of justice as the ruling principle of human society.

Comparative Religions 103
Essay: BAHA'I
Eleanor Byrne

In an essay for a religion course, one ought to be fair and dispassionate. Yet I must begin this essay on Baha'i with a personal history; otherwise I would have to hide my real concerns and just describe the Baha'i faith. It is because I feel so drawn toward this religion—almost as if a hand is touching my shoulder and a voice is saying, "This is it. This is what you have always been looking for"—that I write this less-than-objective presentation.

Raised as I was, a missionary's child in Africa, I was disturbed, even at a young age, by the knowledge that my parents' work centered around getting local tribespeople to leave their traditional beliefs in order to learn the "new" faith of Christianity. What if something these people believed was true, only we just didn't know it? I often worried about that question.

Later in high school I studied African history. The teacher explained as best he could the difference between universal and particular religions. A certain tribe, for example, would think of its particular religion as relevant only to the people in that tribe. But those who held to a universal religion believed their one religion was the only correct one and that any other religion was a false religion. The teacher told us the universal religions were Christianity, Judaism, and Islam. I doubt whether he knew much about Baha'i; at least he never mentioned it.

That class started me wondering how three religions could each claim to be the only true one. At first that wasn't too hard; I could just say that as a Christian I knew Christianity was the truth and that the followers of the other religions were misguided into evil substitutes. But in the middle of that same school year I dated a Muslim student for a couple of months. He was a pretty modern guy, partly educated in England, and serious enough about the Islam faith to make me realize a couple of things.

First, many Muslims are tremendously serious about serving God. And second, I as a Christian could agree

RELIGIONS ARE SPIRITUALLY ONE

Religions that have resulted from the lives and teachings of God's Manifestations form a spiritual unity although their outward forms are different.

Each Manifestation adds the new social teachings and laws necessary for the new Age. These are temporary and subject to periods of development and decay. The spiritual teachings, however, are eternal.

All men who worship God are one in the unity of spirit.

Because of this unity, Bahaullah teaches that religion separates mankind by causing disunity
It Is Not Expressing the Spirit of God.

As the Manifestations are spiritually one, so religion is one.
Harmony and Unity Express the Will of God.

Ray Meyer, *Baha'i, Follower of the Light,* p. 21

41

IF YOU ARE OF
ANOTHER FAITH

*To Christians, becoming a Baha'i
does not mean renouncing Christ.*

Christ and Bahaullah are
Spiritually One.

*To Muslims, becoming a Baha'i
does not mean renouncing
Muhammad.*

Muhammad and Bahaullah are
Spiritually One.

*The same applies to Krishna,
Moses, Zoroaster, Buddha
and the Bab.*

*Baha'is who come from a
Christian background find that
their love for and understanding of
Christ deepens. His teachings
continue to enrich their lives.*

Bahaullah
*leads them to all truth......
as Christ promised.*

*They also find new interest in
other Faiths and thus gain from
the wonderful richness of God's
revelation as it has been expressed
in other times and places.*

This is One of the Wonders of
Baha'i.

*For those who come to Baha'i from
other religious backgrounds, the
same thing applies.*

*Baha'i fulfils all Faiths without
destroying any. This is a test of its
truthfulness. God's oneness is
confirmed.*

Ray Meyer, *Baha'i, Follower of the Light*, p. 45

with more of the major truths I heard from the lips of Muslims than I would have suspected. I was particularly surprised to realize that Muslims revere Jesus and consider him a major prophet.

The above experiences started me on the track upon which I am slowly progressing. At least I *hope* it is progress. (I know some of my friends have been upset by me and still are.) Over and over I've been asking myself the same questions: if Jews and Christians and Muslims all serve the same God who created us all, and if none of our religions is absolutely perfect, why should we Christians try to convince the others to become like us? Isn't God able to tell who his children are among the Jews or Muslims—or even among the pagans? And why, oh why, are wars fought over these issues?

In high school the general attitude was that those questions were wrong, so I tried to shut up. But I never was really content. When I graduated and came to North America, I decided on Bible college—not to be a missionary like my folks are hoping, but to see if there really were any reasons why Christianity could claim to be "right and true" over against all other religions. I was hoping to find some answers.

And now since I've come across Baha'i in this class, it looks like a completely different answer is building up in my mind. Baha'i is a religion that claims to be universal. But it is not just a fourth universal religion. Instead of knocking or attacking the other major faiths, Baha'i accepts them. It accepts Moses and Jesus and Mohammed and shows how each of them was truly showing us the way to God—though doing so in terms of his particular time and place. It shows how the time was ripe for a new messenger of God to come and fulfill all these faiths in order to save not just individual souls but the whole human race.

Bahaullah, the messenger of God who wrote most of the Baha'i scriptures, taught the most peaceful doctrines I have ever encountered. Almost everything I stand for is included in the beliefs of the church: justice for all, no prejudice, no nationalism, equality of men and women, agreement between religion and science. I could go on, but the point is that this church preaches what I've always been taught to recognize as "the fruits of the Spirit."

As to the central doctrine of Christianity, here is what one Baha'i writer has said:

Bahaullah...fully confirms the teachings of Christ and no person is permitted to become a Baha'i without first acknowledging Christ Jesus as the Word made flesh...and the Son of God.

I realize from my own study of Christianity that Jesus went up to heaven and promised he would come again. Bahaullah, the founder of Baha'i, is believed to be the fulfillment of the second coming, bringing to humanity the new revelations for this age.

And our age certainly needs these revelations. I remember the shock I received when I came back from Africa to find my local church liked to entertain black visitors from other countries—but didn't want to invite local black people to their services. Not long after that, a half-dozen families left that congregation because they were dissatisfied with something the church decided regarding communion. They joined another denomination and now everybody's angry at them.

But Bahaullah teaches:

The religion of God...hath been revealed...for the sake of union and harmony among the people of the world; make it not a means for disagreement and discord! (Bahaullah, *Baha'i World Faith,* p. 201)

And about racism he says:

Prejudice and fanaticism whether sectarian, denominational, patriotic or political are destructive to the foundations of human solidarity; therefore man should release himself from such bonds in order that the oneness of the world of humanity may become manifest. (Bahaullah, *Baha'i World Faith,* p. 247)

In John 16:12–13 Jesus said:

"I have yet many things to say to you, but ye cannot bear them now. When the Spirit of truth comes, he will guide you into all the truth. . . ."

I recognize so many truths in Baha'i that I feel I ought to ask myself seriously: is Baha'i the fulfillment of the truths of all religions? If it is, ought I not to associate with its followers and perhaps become one?

BAHAULLAH

Bahaullah is the central figure of the Baha'i Faith. Through Him God has once again revealed Himself to mankind.

Bahaullah is God's Manifestation for this age and is Spiritually one with Krishna, Moses, Zoroaster, Buddha, Christ, Muhammad, the Bab and the other Manifestations of the past.

Through Bahaullah mankind is being spiritually renewed and a new world civilization is arising.

Acceptance of Bahaullah and His teachings is the supreme challenge to modern man.

Bahaullah suffered in order to fulfil Christ's promise that God's Kingdom will be established on Earth as it is in Heaven.

Ray Meyer, *Baha'i, Follower of the Light,* p. 9

MAN—ONE FAMILY

A new day in the history of
mankind has already dawned,

The World Is Now
One World.

*Since Bahaullah gave His
teachings to the world there have
been over a hundred years of
progress towards racial equality.
The Baha'i Faith has influenced
the formation of the League of
Nations, which has been followed
by the United Nations in which
there is no discrimination between
the representatives of any race. The
Universal Declaration of Human
Rights and other statements and
aims of the United Nations also
embody Baha'i principles.*

*A beautiful thing about Baha'is is
their delight in racial and cultural
differences. People from all over
the world welcome and respect each
other and work together with
utmost harmony.*

*In a marriage between people of
different races and cultures the
essential thing is the love and
respect that each has for the other.*

*In the Baha'i Faith, those whose
hearts have been set aglow by the
energizing influence of God's love,
cherish people as people and
recognize in their differences the
signs of God's reflected glory.*

Ray Meyer, *Baha'i, Follower of the Light,* p. 23

I realize I was supposed to write a historical analysis of the emergence of Baha'i as a world faith, and instead I just dwelt on my own questions. I could have recounted Baha'i's early Persian history and the struggles of the Bab, the prophet who prepared the way for Bahaullah. But I hope you'll forgive me for writing about what concerned me more—my own reactions to the Baha'i faith.

FOR FURTHER READING

Van Baalen, J. K. *The Chaos of Cults.* Grand Rapids, Mich.: Eerdmans Publishing Company, 1962.

Offers a short treatment of Baha'i (pp. 146–61).

Information about the Baha'i faith can be obtained from the Baha'i center in your city or from National Baha'i Headquarters, 536 Sheridan Road, Wilmette, Illinois 60091.

CASSETTE TAPES

Martin, Walter. *The World of the Cults,* Vol. 2. Includes Bahaism, Black Muslims, Scientology, Hare Krishna, and others (six cassettes). C-18. Available from the Christian Research Institute, Box 500, San Juan Capistrano, California 92693. Write for current prices and brochure.

Baha'i—One Universal Faith

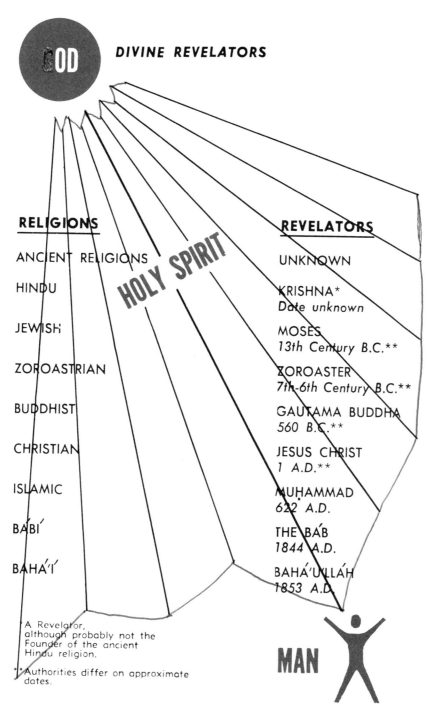

GOD

DIVINE REVELATORS

RELIGIONS

ANCIENT RELIGIONS

HINDU

JEWISH

ZOROASTRIAN

BUDDHIST

CHRISTIAN

ISLAMIC

BÁBÍ

BAHÁ'Í

HOLY SPIRIT

REVELATORS

UNKNOWN

KRISHNA*
Date unknown

MOSES
13th Century B.C.**

ZOROASTER
7th-6th Century B.C.**

GAUTAMA BUDDHA
560 B.C.**

JESUS CHRIST
1 A.D.**

MUHAMMAD
622 A.D.

THE BÁB
1844 A.D.

BAHÁ'U'LLÁH
1853 A.D.

*A Revelator,
although probably not the
Founder of the ancient
Hindu religion.

**Authorities differ on approximate
dates.

MAN

SESSION GUIDE

CHALLENGE 3 BAHA'I—THE CHILDREN OF LIGHT

A. Personal notes/questions on Challenge 3

B. The Baha'i challenge

1. Try this true/false quiz on Baha'i.

_T_ a. Baha'i finds some revealed truth in nearly all major religions.

_T_ b. If you, as a Christian, talked about your faith, a Baha'i would probably agree with most of what you said.

_F_ c. Baha'i denies the divinity of Jesus Christ.

_F_ d. As a Baha'i, you would look forward to the second coming of Christ.

_F_ e. As a Baha'i, you would have to accept the absolute authority of Bahaullah as a prophet, equal to Christ, bringing God's latest and most complete revelation.

_F_ f. As a Baha'i, you would be an independent seeker after truth and would seldom, if ever, meet with other Baha'is.

_F_ g. The single, most important Baha'i belief is in humanity's sinfulness and need for salvation.

_T_ h. The moral principles that govern a Baha'i's daily life are ones Christians should also support.

_T_ i. Baha'i, although begun in Iran in the nineteenth century, is a worldwide religion today.

_T_ j. Baha'i would be critical of Christianity's division into numerous denominations and sects.

_F_ k. Baha'is are readily identifiable by their weird clothing and general appearance.

_F_ l. One of the reasons Baha'i has grown so rapidly is the intensive, high-pressure, door-to-door witnessing of its members.

2. What does Baha'i offer that many modern people find so attractive?

C. The Christian response

   1. From the Christian perspective, in what general area is Baha'i most vulnerable to criticism?

   Chris is ~~our~~ our redemer and Baha' does not. Chris is num. 1 to us bat not to them

   2. What Bible passages might you cite to refute Baha'i's teaching about Bahaullah? See if you can find at least two.

   (Act 4: 12, Act1: 11B, John 14: 6, Romeas 3: 43, Hebews 8:7)

   3. Optional: Reflect briefly on your church's confessions about Christ being the only Savior. (See Heidelberg Catechism Q & A 30; Belgic Confession, Article XXII; Canons of Dort, Second Head of Doctrine; or other confessions your church has adopted.)

   4. How would you witness to a Baha'i about your Christian faith? What approach would you take to convince him or her of your beliefs?

L. Ron Hubbard Experimenting with "Hubbard E-Meter"

THE CHURCH OF SCIENTOLOGY

Founding: In 1950 science fiction writer L. Ron Hubbard wrote a book called *Dianetics: The Modern Science of Mental Health.* In 1952 he founded the *Hubbard Association of Scientologists* as a research foundation. In 1954 Scientology became a religion when Hubbard established the *Founding Church of Scientology* in Washington, D.C. The "Flag Land Base" of the movement is in Clearwater, Florida.

Following: The Church of Scientology claims three million adherents in North America, five million adherents worldwide. It has been banned in Australia and for a number of years England banned foreign Scientologists and refused visas to students who wished to enter the country to study Scientology.

Faith: *The mind, which controls the brain, has two parts: the analytic and reactive. The analytic (conscious) mind works with precision unless it's upset by engrams (sensory impression of past shock events) recorded in the reactive (unconscious) mind.
   *In Dianetic Reverie an auditor (therapist) with the help of an E-meter (an electronic device which detects engrams) is able to help a pre-Clear (patient) to recall forgotten shock incidents and thus push the engrams out of the reactive mind and become "Clear."
   *Each person's real "you" is a fallen immortal god (Thetan). The Thetans created the universe out of matter, energy, space, and

time (MEST) but, by voluntarily handicapping themselves and limiting their knowledge, became trapped in the material universe, forgetting their innate and rightful deity and coming to think they were bodies.

*Each Thetan has been reincarnated over trillions of years and carries in her reactive mind all the engrams of these earlier existences.

*By removing the engrams of these million previous lifetimes, a person can first become "Clear" and then advance to the level of Operating Thetan, free from all the problems of MEST and gifted with almost miraculous powers.

2434 Menominee Drive
Portland, Oregon
Thursday, November 5

Sam Beach
1012 Walnut Street
Vancouver, British Columbia

Dear Sam,

I've no real excuse for not writing you earlier except that I had nothing much to write about for quite a while—all of last year, in fact, was a bummer. And I'll admit it, I was embarrassed to write you at all. Now things are different and I'll give it a try.

Remember the "heavy talks" we had just before graduation? Ironic, isn't it—I was going to be the first Ph.D. from our high school and you were either going to enlist or be a bum. (I forget which was your first choice!) And now *you're* the one who's pursuing a big career. Even when you graduate, I don't guarantee I'll let you work on my teeth!

Your sister gave me your address. She told me you knew I'd dropped out of school and that it had come as quite a shock to you. I'm not surprised you were surprised—I had a 3.5 when I decided I couldn't go on. There was just no way. Now I can explain most of it, but at the time I couldn't make any sense out of anything.

What frustrated me was what I call fragmentation. If I tried to bring some history into the math class, or some questions about Freud into the Bible class, the instructor would become as near to offended as a Christian college will permit. It didn't take me long to realize I was looking for a more complete, rounded view of reality, one that could account for everything, including why I felt so frustrated with myself. So I dropped out and—following your lead—hit the road!

The reason I can write now is that I have found what I was looking for: a system of thought that takes everything into account. I've found a new way of looking at life—all because I decided to skip a movie in downtown Portland and cross a street to skim the material in the window of the Church of Scientology reading room.

Don't worry; I haven't dropped Christianity or lost my faith. Scientology leaves one free to define God in whatever way one wishes. But it does add to my understanding of how everything fits together in this world.

For one thing, I never could make anything out of Hindu myths and theories of reincarnation or how that could fit with, say, Freud's ideas about the subconscious, or the Christian idea of the soul. But Scientology has insights into all of that and more.

Take the soul. I couldn't distinguish it from the mind before. But now I see that my soul is the part of me that is really me, my life force. We call the soul the Thetan. The mind is different: it stores up all the mental pictures that the soul or Thetan records.

Freud wasn't too far off when he divided the mind into the conscious and the subconscious. Scientologists agree that the mind has two parts. The *analytical* mind is the part we use when we are thinking clearly. And the *reactive* mind contains all the unconscious and painful images and pictures from the millions of past existences the Thetan evolved through until he inhabited this body I call me.

Don't laugh too quickly, Sam. How many times haven't you had some funny thing happen which upset you *all out of proportion* to its real significance—and you didn't know why. Scientologists will tell you it was an *engram,* and you were reacting to a painful copy of something that happened to you in the millions of years of your Thetan's past history. These engrams can be removed by proper pastoral counseling, leaving you free from the kinds of things you'd call tension or frustration. This is a big job since some of the engrams may have been recorded by the Thetan even trillions of years ago.

The pastor is trained in how to use an electrometer to measure the slightest tension you might feel when his questions or suggestions touch upon an engram in your reactive mind. When they are discovered, you can rid the mind of them. And when they are all expelled, you are "Clear." That's sort of like being a saint in Christian terms. What I really like are the definitions and explanations that help one grasp what's going on. Here's an example:

Before a computer can be used to solve a problem, it must be cleared of all previous solutions and data. Otherwise it will unconsciously add the old solution into the new one and produce irrational behavior and inability. Auditing "clears" more and more of these hidden decisions from the functioning mind.

Notice the up-to-date terminology? Instead of talking about *pastoral counseling,* Scientologists use the word *auditing.* I appreciate that—almost as much as I respect and appreciate the person responsible for it: the fantastic man who founded Scientology, L. Ron Hubbard. Hubbard traveled all over the world as a young child and earned several degrees before he entered the military. While he was in the navy, he cured himself of grave injuries; even the doctors couldn't explain how it had happened. When he left the military, he started writing. In fact, he was a famous author long before he decided to develop the various theories that led to Scientology. Even now he spends his time in research and writing—though he no longer administers the church.

Yes, Scientology is a church, though it doesn't compete with Christianity or other faiths. It holds services and does a lot of work in social reforms. I'm enclosing some literature. Remembering some of our high school talks, I really think you'd find this exciting. And it's fun! You feel yourself relaxing and enjoying your real self as you get closer to "Clear." I've a ways to go yet, and I have to get a little more money together to keep going for counseling. But I love every minute of it.

I hope you are as satisfied with your progress in life as I am with mine. But if you feel anything like I did when I dropped out of school, look up the Church of Scientology and go in for a free interview; the address is on the material I'm enclosing.

Now that I've brought you up-to-date regarding myself, I'll wait for your reply—it'd be nice to get a dialogue going like we used to.

Sincerely,
Alan Miller

There is no name to describe the way I feel.
At last I am cause. I am Clear—I can do anything I want to do. I feel like a child with a new life— everything is so wonderful and beautiful.

Clear is Clear!

It's unlike anything I could have imagined. The colors, the clarity, the brightness of everything is beyond belief. Everything is so new, I feel new born. I am filled with the wonder of everything.

Robert Ellwood, *Religious and Spiritual Groups in Modern America,* p. 168

FOR FURTHER READING

Ellwood, Robert. *Religious and Spiritual Groups in Modern America.* Englewood Cliffs, N.J.: Prentice Hall, 1973.

Features an objective chapter on Scientology.

Gruss, Edward Charles. *Cults and the Occult in the Age of Aquarius.* Nutley, N.J.: Presbyterian and Reformed Publishing Co., 1974.

Newport, John P. *Christ and the New Consciousness.* Nashville: Broadman Press, 1978.

Offers a chapter of background on Ron Hubbard, basic teachings of Scientology, outreach and recruiting methods, secular and theological criticism.

Scientology: A World Religion Emerges in the Space Age. Hollywood, Calif.: Church of Scientology Information Service, 1974.

Scientology as seen by those who believe it.

Wallis, Roy. *The Road to Total Freedom: A Sociological Analysis of Scientology.* New York: Columbia University Press, 1977.

Has an unusual view of the distinction between sect and cult and applies this to Scientology, but does contain a good deal of information based on a study of documents and interviews with members.

CASSETTE TAPES

Martin, Walter. *Scientology.* C-92. Available from the Christian Research Institute, Box 500, San Juan Capistrano, California 92693. Write for current prices and brochure.

E-Meter Used to Detect Engrams

FRED GRANT

SESSION GUIDE

CHALLENGE 4   THE CHURCH OF SCIENTOLOGY

A. Personal notes/questions on Challenge 4

B. Challenge and response

How would you respond to Alan's letter? Would you attack Scientology as a cultic ripoff? Would you tend to agree with Alan that Scientology is a legitimate, useful religion which does not conflict with Christianity?

Use the space below to write a brief letter of response to Alan Miller (from Sam's point of view). You may dispense with the normal pleasantries and get right to the issue!

Dear Alan,

It would make you forget about Christianity.

Sincerely,
Sam Beach

Compare your letter with those of your classmates and with the letter printed in Response 4. Jot new ideas in the space below.

Hare Krishna Procession

CHALLENGE 5

HARE KRISHNA

Founding: The International Society for Krishna Consciousnses (ISKCON), was founded in the United States in 1966 by His Divine Grace A. C. De Bhaktivedanta Swami Prabhupada, an Indian businessman who had been told by his spiritual master thirty years earlier that he should preach the news of Krishna in English to the West. When he arrived in North America, Prabhupada, already in his sixties, preached the orthodox doctrines of a small, conservative Hindu sect that originated in northern India in the fifteenth century.

Following: ISKCON claims 3,000 followers (1972) in 68 centers spread throughout the United States, Canada, and other Western nations. They also claim a circulation of over 500,000 in North America alone for their monthly magazine, *Back to Godhead.* Worldwide circulation of the magazine (which is printed in thirteen languages) is estimated at over 1,000,000. Among those who contributed to the spread of ISKCON, George Harrison of the Beatles stands out. After his song "My Sweet Lord" hit the top of the charts, new Krishna centers sprang up throughout the United States and Canada.

Faith: *There is Absolute Truth in all the great world scriptures (Bible, Koran, Torah, etc.), but the oldest Vedic scriptures, especially the *Bhagavad-gita,* are the literal record of God's actual words.
*Krishna is the Supreme Personality of Godhead himself, the god

of gods, creator and sustainer of all life. Krishna's three paramount attributes are *sat* (bring), *cit* (knowledge), and *ananda* (bliss).

*A human being is not a material body (this is considered the greatest pitfall of life). The real person is a pure spirit, eternal, and part of Krishna.

*The main purpose of life is Krishna consciousness, a pure state of the soul living in blissful loving relationship with Lord Krishna. The easiest way to attain this state is to chant the Hare Krishna mantra (a mystical formula repeated as an act of worship or petition).

*The devotee must follow four rules: no gambling, no intoxicants, no illicit sex, and no eating of meat, fish, or eggs.

*The basic mission of believers is to propagate the *sankirtana* (chanting of the holy names of God) all around the world. Their duty is to chant and dance publicly and thus teach people to love Krishna and worship him in their daily life.

I know what you're thinking, and I don't mind. "What a freak!" you'll say. "Those crazy robes and the shaved head." To you I'm from a million miles away. That's all right. I might have thought a bit like that a couple of years ago myself. Though I never was too hung up about whether or not I fit in.

You'll take my flower and stammer thanks and leave. Kind of embarrassed. That's better than arguing, though. No matter what you'd have said, you would have lost. And you would probably have gotten angry while I simply repeated my mantra and smiled at you. Don't think it's easy to learn to control oneself like that. No one can except the person who's in Krishna consciousness all the time. I just think of His Divine Grace and say my mantra and you really can't get to me. Anyway, how could you understand?

But I think I can understand you. Nice home, nice parents, nice church, nice school, nice friends. Everything nice. I remember a time I thought a bit like that. Everything seemed nice—except my nice parents fought a lot and my nice church was racist (just a little). And my friends were nice too, with nice clothes and bikes and cars. At least they seemed nice until I began to see how much they thought about the nice clothes and cars, which was all the time.

Most of them stayed that way, but I guess I changed. I was looking for something—at first maybe just kicks. The kids who partied seemed to be having more fun than the rest. It didn't take me long to realize I really couldn't handle the drug scene, but by then I was too far gone. At least I was a long way from the nice kids and nice clothes and nice cars.

Drugs are a mistake; I see that now. But in one way at least they put me on the right track. LSD is a fool's game, but it showed me colors and sounds and a kind of deep peace beyond anything I had ever seen or thought or felt before. My problem wasn't with what it did for me—just that I couldn't control how much of anything I took or when. I think now that I wasn't an addict for the *drug* but for the experiences themselves.

Playing with drugs has rules too, I found out. And I followed them all: hit the street, sleep around, steal,

The life-style of most devotees prior to entrance into ISKCON can be described as permissive with regard to work, drugs, and sexual mores. Most described their predevotee lives to me as a psychedelic drop-out process. . .preconversion drug experiences are viewed by most devotees as temporary but life altering events.

Francine J. Daner, "Conversion to Krishna Consciousness: The Transformation from Hippie to Religious Ascetic" (Roy Wallis, *Sectarianism*, p. 55)

By sincerely cultivating a bona fide spiritual science, we can be free from anxiety and come to a state of pure, unending blissful consciousness in this lifetime.

A short statement of the philosophy of Krsna Consciousness, *Back to Godhead,* Vol. 11, No. 5, p. 10

Lord Krsna's beauty possesses mind-attracting splendor greater than emeralds.

Back to Godhead, Vol. 11, No. 5, p. 11

and just feel sick all through your body. If I could choose between returning to what I was like then or becoming like you, I'd choose to be straight as a pin. Fortunately, I met some members of the Krishna Consciousness movement when I was really down. Just the fact that they smiled made them look okay to me. They told me they could give me more than a meal: they could show me how to stay off drugs and stay high at the same time. When they said "stay high on God," I have to admit *I* thought they were a little crazy.

I went with them to their temple, had the meal, and stayed the night. Nothing religious, I thought, though now I see that the meal had been offered to Krishna. He was in the food I ate just as he is now in everything I say and do. But at the time all I wanted was an answer to the drug thing.

And they had that all right. Krishna is his name, I learned, and just to say the name is to participate, if only a little, in Krishna consciousness. The mantra celebrates his name. We sang the mantra—chanted it hundreds of times in the first few days. Now it's always in the back of my mind. *Hare Krishna, Hare Krishna, Krishna, Krishna, Hare Hare, Hare Rama, Hare Rama, Rama Rama, Hare Hare.* The chant means: "O all-attractive, all-pleasing Lord, O energy of the Lord, please engage me in Your devotional service."

But the translation's not as important as the sounds of the words themselves. The repetition of them frees me from my improper concern and worry about the things around me. And, as His Divine Grace says, we live in the age of quarrel. Even you ought to be able to see that's true.

Quarrels and arguments—I had enough of that as a child to last a hundred lifetimes. Maybe in a previous existence I had resisted God and deserved to go through a lot before Krishna sent his messenger to me. But I don't argue anymore. Srila Prabhupada is truly one with Krishna in his understanding of everything. To submit to his teaching is to submit to the truth. Then you see how you are part of the truth and there's no need to argue.

So I struggle every day to focus on Krishna. I can be

honest with you. I sometimes get tired. There are a lot of rules: no silly games, no gambling, no coffee or tea or strong drinks, no acts of sexual impurity, no eating of meat or fish or eggs. I'm probably stricter than the strictest religious friends you have. But that's the only way to learn something completely, and the study of God and how we are part of him is worth learning as fully as I can.

I think the clothing and the initiation service and the new name I have all help. Otherwise I'd still be Mike Greer, trying to pretend I'd left my former lifestyle, but always thinking I could go back to it. Instead, it's almost as if I've left that whole person behind. I gave all my money (the little I had) to the movement. And now all I own are some books, the clothes I'm wearing, some beads, a sleeping bag, and a watch. I've left everything else behind and I don't miss it.

I can see now how much I was really owned by things. I had really fallen far, and so I've got a long way to go. But it's not something I have to do alone. With drugs and the whole Hippie scene, you're on your own—no one really cares if you succeed or fail. But it's exactly the opposite here. As I was learning my way, hardly able to do more than chant the mantra, my brothers and sisters were helping me every step of the way. I could easily see why I was considered polluted and dangerous, but that didn't make them scorn me or ignore me. They showed me how to rid myself of old thought patterns—and it won't be long now before I'm ready for my second ceremony! I'll become a brahmin! I'll have my secret mantra, and I may get opportunities to perform some of the ceremonies.

I know it's not easy, but I'm sure I'll be in Krishna the rest of my life. Many moments of the day I'm aware of how my old self tries to come back and of how impure my devotion to Krishna is. But when I really surrender to Krishna and let him take over, I see myself just disappear. I see how I am a part of him, and how the disgusting person I have been is part of an illusion because I wasn't concentrating on devotion to God.

I suppose you have saintly old men in your church.

I was actually looking for a spiritual master. In my LSD experiences and my other life experiences I had come to the point where I didn't know what the truth was. I was looking for someone to tell me. . . . When I read Srila Prabhupada's books I could see that he was a person who knew every place where I was at and had been on these LSD trips and something far beyond which I couldn't fathom.

Francine J. Daner, "Conversion to Krishna Consciousness: The Transformation from Hippie to Religious Ascetic" (Roy Wallis, *Sectarianism*, p. 53)

There's an old Bengali proverb that seems to explain my good fortune very nicely: "By the grace of Krsna, you get your spiritual master. And by the grace of your spiritual master, you get Krsna."

Yadubara dasa (John Griesser) describing the details of his conversion to Hare Krishna. *Back to Godhead*, Vol. 11, No. 5, p. 24

. . . Out of His compassion the Supreme Lord not only manifests Himself as the guru *within, but also appears externally in the world as the pure devotee of God or the spiritual master in disciplic succession. Krsna as the Supersoul is within a person's heart, and when one is serious, the Lord directs him to take shelter of His representative, a genuine spiritual master. Directed from within and guided externally by the self-realized spiritual master, one attains the path of Krsna consciousness, the way out of material suffering.*

Satsvarupa dasa Goswami, *Back to Godhead*, Vol. 14, No. 10, p. 32

Among us, persons who have attained consciousness of Krishna to a specially high level are the *sannyasas*. They have special tasks and travel about, studying the scriptures and preaching. I would like to be a *sannyasa*.

But you wouldn't understand that. You would probably laugh if I asked you if you wanted to be a saint. But I see what I was before Krishna gave me a master, and before the master gave me Krishna. I don't think you really see yourself as you are yet. Maybe you never will.

FOR FURTHER READING

Back to Godhead (the magazine of the Hare Krishna movement)

    A monthly magazine published by the Bhaktivedanta Book Trust, 3764 Watseka Ave., Los Angeles, California 90034

Daner, Francine Jeanne. *The American Children of Krsna: A Study of the Hare Krsna Movement.* New York: Holt, Rinehart and Winston, 1976.

    Offers an excellent, thorough analysis of the movement.

Sparks, Jack. *The Mind Benders.* Nashville: Thomas Nelson, Inc., 1977.

    Features a thirty-page chapter on the history and theology of Hare Krishna, their method of operation, and a refutation from a Christian perspective.

Yamamoto, Isamu. *Hare Krishna, Hare Krishna.* Downers Grove, Ill.: Inter-Varsity Press, 1978.

    A short, very helpful book with information on the background, leader, and doctrines of Hare Krishna.

CASSETTE TAPES

Martin, Walter. *The World of the Cults.* Vol. 2. Includes Bahaism, Black Muslims, Scientology, Hare Krishna, and others (six cassettes). C-18. Available from Christian Research Institute, Box 500, San Juan Capistrano, California 92693. Write for current prices and brochure.

Hare Krishna Student

SESSION GUIDE

CHALLENGE 5   HARE KRISHNA

A. Personal notes/questions on Challenge 5

B. Challenge and response

Mike Greer would be more than eager to talk with you about your beliefs and his. But what would you talk about? What do Hare Krishna and Christianity have in common?

Solution - caunfer in life.
the cete of retery em
God's Authority

Review the *Common Ground* approach outlined at the back of your textbook. Then see if you can find at least three truths or perspectives on the world which Christianity seems to have in common with Hare Krishna. For each idea in common, explain briefly how the Christian position is a more complete, broader truth.

C. Role-play

Setting: quiet corner of a local airport

Situation: Mike Greer (the Hare Krishna) is talking with a Christian. So far the Christian has been mostly listening to Greer explain his views (as in Challenge 5). Now the Christian decides to try the *Common Ground* approach, or something close to it. Greer listens but is free to interrupt whenever he has a criticism to make, a question to ask, and so on. The Christian begins...

The Zodiac

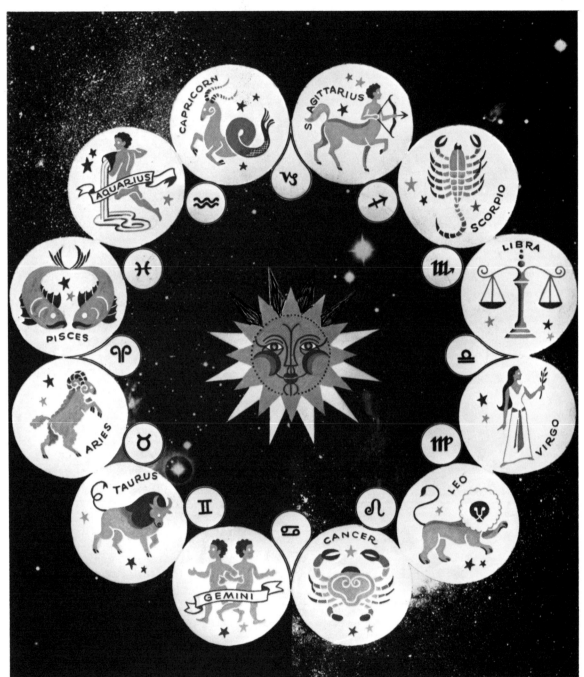

CHALLENGE 6

ASTROLOGY

Founding: Modern astrology comes from the ancient Babylonians. Other systems of astrology developed in China, India, and in what is now the Americas.

Following: It is estimated that in the United States there are about 10,000 professional and 175,000 amateur astrologers. About 5 million people plan their lives according to astrological predictions while over 20 million consult astrologers from time to time. US polls show over 20 percent of the population believe in astrology, 24 percent read astrological columns daily, and over 77 percent know their astrological sign. Interest and belief is about the same in Canada and greater in Great Britain, France, and Germany.

Faith: *There is a universal order of the universe expressed in the order of the stars.
*The fixed stars, sun, moon, and planets have a decisive influence on people and things, and the position of these at the time of a person's birth will determine that person's character, personality, and ultimate destiny.
*By casting and interpreting a horoscope an expert can show where, when, and how a person will be lucky (favorable and unfavorable indications), how to take advantage of lucky opportunities, how to increase one's luck, and how to avoid bad luck.

The following article is excerpted from *Hermes' Worker,* the monthly magazine distributed to the employees of Hermes' Trucks, Inc.

Amateur Astrologer on the Dock

Harvey Willard has worked on the Hermes' main terminal dock as a freight checker for the past two years. He agreed to share this information with the *Hermes' Worker.* The material presented here was taken from a tape-recorded interview with reporter Bob Anderson.

I know some people might get angry when I say I prefer my horoscope to my Bible, but I think I can explain that. I still use them both, but for different things. The horoscope just naturally gets the most use.

I got into astrology about a year and a half ago when a friend of mine really got lucky—he quit his job and a day later had another that paid twice as much. When I asked him how he dared do that (when he quit he had no idea of what he would do next) he told me that his horoscope had told him to expect things to change for the better during the next week. Because the one thing he didn't like was the job he had then, he quit the same day. And things happened just like the horoscope said they would.

At that same time I was a little frustrated with my home and church. There were some personal things I wanted advice on—I wasn't married then—and everyone quoted verses from the Bible at me. Trouble is, they used the same verses to make different points. And no one could come straight out and tell me what to do. It was all *maybe this* and *maybe that.*

So when my friend put me on to astrology, I read a few things about it in the newspaper and even sent for some stuff by mail. And I found out an important difference between the Bible and astrology. They don't really contradict each other—they sort of help fill each other out.

It's like this—the Bible answers all the *big* questions: Who made us? How did we become sinful? Who will save us? Where are we going after we die? But it doesn't say much about the little, everyday questions—

Astrology comes from two words, astro (star) and logos (word), and means "word from the stars" or the message of the stars to us.

Leon McBeth, *Strange New Religions,* p. 80

like whether you should change jobs or whether you can afford to get married or not.

Astrology works in real nice here because it doesn't disagree with the Bible. There's no new god or any doctrines to agree or disagree with. It's just a way to get a better idea of all those little questions: Should I take a vacation in June or August? Should I invest in some oil stocks or just keep my money in a bank? Where would you find an answer to questions like that in the Bible?

Astrology can even help you understand yourself better. The Bible talks a lot about Joseph, Moses, Jesus, Paul, and a lot of others who were big in past history. I don't knock their importance, but what about you and me? Where does it talk about Bob Anderson? How does each one of us fit in?

Again, astrology can help out here. Do you know what a natal horoscope is? It's a description of the exact position of the sun, moon, and planets in relation to both the zodiac and the time and place you were born. Each person's is different, of course, because no one is born at exactly the same time and place. From that description a lot can be said about the sort of personality and potentials you start off with in life.

That may not completely explain why you are where you are today (a lot of other things have as much influence on what happens to you as the stars do) but it sure can help. In my case there was a combination of fiery planets in the air when I was born. That means I have a fiery personality. But it's pretty well-balanced, too, because my planets are fixed, cardinal, and mutable. And because three angles are tenanted by planets, I can be sure of my strength. Which probably explains why I like dock work.

I'm not so foolish as to think that my natal horoscope explains everything. My heredity and environment have a lot to do with what I am. And the daily position of the stars, sun, moon, and planets are important to each individual too. But knowing my horoscope has really helped me understand myself a little more than I did before. Now I find it easier to make the daily decisions I have to make—because I know more about my-

[Astrology will soon be] an adjunct to psychology and psychiatry, [because it is] much more complex and sophisticated than present psychological maps or systems.

Dr. Ralph L. Metzner, Stanford University psychologist. *Time*, March 21, 1969

Your natal horoscope is covered by a one year—365 day—full money back guarantee.

John F. Ford, President, The American Astrological Association (from a newspaper ad)

*Every twenty years, astrologers tell
us, Saturn and Uranus come close
to each other in the heavens—an
event known as conjunction.
During the past one hundred years
every president inaugurated in the
year of conjunction has died in
office: Lincoln, 1861; Garfield,
1881; McKinley, 1901; Harding,
1921; Roosevelt, 1941; and
Kennedy, 1961. Four out of the six
were murdered.*

Landmarks, Vol. III, No. 5

self and how I fit into this world.

I make pretty good money on the dock, but I'm not the type to spend it foolishly. I know some people pay out a small fortune to have a weekly or monthly horoscope prepared especially for them. I read somewhere that there are more than ten thousand fulltime astrologists working in the United States. That means an awful lot of people must use them. I wonder if there are ten thousand fulltime ministers of Christian churches in the states.

Anyway, I'm not actually spending a lot of money on it because I'm training myself. There's a lot more to astrology than just reading the column in the daily newspaper. I first got some books from the local library and read them. Then I sent for an astrological kit —which was really just some atlases and some books of tables giving positions of planets for each day in the year.

It can get pretty complicated. There's more to astrology than filling out facts in the horoscope blanks; you've also got to interpret the significance of that information. But using your common sense can go quite a ways.

I do horoscopes for my friends now. I don't charge anything yet because I'm still learning and I can't guarantee my interpretations are as good as the experts'. But like everything else, practice makes perfect. So for any of my friends who don't come soon, it may cost a bit!

I'd recommend astrology for anyone. Like I said, I'm a Christian and I don't find it conflicts with church or anything. You can add astrology to whatever you believe because it's not about God. But it *is* one of the older ways of learning things about yourself. It may not be as true a science as medicine or physics, but in my own experience it can be just as helpful.

FOR FURTHER READING

Bayly, Joseph. *What About Horoscopes.* Elgin, Ill.: David C. Cook Publishing Co., 1970.

Gross, Edmond Charles. *Cults and the Occult in the Age of Aquarius.* Nutley, N. J.: Presbyterian and Reformed Publishing Co., 1974.

  Features a chapter on astrology, addressing such questions as whether or not it works, whether or not it is supported by Scripture, and so on.

McBeth, Leon. *Strange New Religions.* Nashville: Broadman Press, 1977.

  Offers a chapter which includes a capsule history of astrology, a logical refutation, and evaluation from the Christian perspective.

Montgomery, John Warwick. *Principalities and Powers.* Minneapolis: Bethany Fellowship, 1973.

CASSETTE TAPES

Martin, Walter. *World of the Occult.* Vol. 1. Includes the Occult Revolution, Witchcraft and Satanism, Astrology, Danger in the Stars, the Doctrines of Demons, Jean Dixon, and others (six cassettes). C-20. Available from the Christian Research Institute, Box 500, San Juan Capistrano, California 92693. Write for current prices and brochure.

Signs of the Zodiac

ARIES —The Ram, Mar. 21–Apr. 19
    (Governs the head)
Mars, Pluto—rulers of the 1st house

Positive: Enterprising, incisive, spontaneous
Negative: Impatient, impetuous
Career: Pioneer, architect, soldier

TAURUS —The Bull, Apr. 20–May 20
    (Governs the neck)
Venus—ruler of the 2nd house

Positive: Determined, practical, kindhearted
Negative: Materialistic, pigheaded, self-indulgent
Career: Builder, producer

GEMINI —The Twins, May 21–June 21
    (Governs the arms and lungs)
Mercury—ruler of the 3rd house

Positive: Mentally energetic, versatile, artistic, witty
Negative: Fickle, dilettantish
Career: Thinker, writer, artist

CANCER —The Crab, June 22–July 22
    (Governs the breast and stomach)
Moon—ruler of the 4th house

Positive: Tenacious, patient, sensitive, persuasive
Negative: Moody, unforgiving
Career: Teacher, salesman

LEO —The Lion, July 23–Aug. 22
    (Governs the heart)
Sun—ruler of the 5th house

Positive: Proud, magnanimous, self-aware
Negative: Egotistical, violent
Career: Leader, politician, entertainer

VIRGO —The Virgin, Aug. 23–Sept. 22
    (Governs the bowels)
Mercury—ruler of the 6th house

Positive: Discriminating, serving, methodical
Negative: Nitpicking, quarrelsome
Career: Critic, craftsman

LIBRA —The Scales, Sept. 23–Oct. 23
    (Governs the kidneys and buttocks)
Venus—ruler of the 7th house

Positive: Balanced, alert, diplomatic, just
Negative: Indecisive, indiscriminating, lazy
Career: Statesman, manager, judge

SCORPIO —The Scorpion, Oct. 24–Nov. 21
    (Governs the sex organs)
Mars, Pluto—rulers of the 8th house

Positive: Intense, emotional, staminal, shrewd
Negative: Sarcastic, vindictive
Career: Investigator, doctor, mystic

SAGITTARIUS —The Archer, Nov. 22–Dec. 21
    (Governs the thighs)
Jupiter—ruler of the 9th house

Positive: Aspiring, curious, nature-loving, athletic
Negative: Discourteous, lacks focus
Career: Lawyer, publisher, traveler

CAPRICORN —The Goat, Dec. 22–Jan. 19
    (Governs the knees)
Saturn—ruler of the 10th house

Positive: Steadfast, reserved, traditional, ambitious
Negative: Snobbish, unscrupulous, selfish
Career: Ambassador, ruler, organizer, religious

AQUARIUS —The Waterman, Jan. 20–Feb. 18
    (Governs the legs and ankles)
Saturn, Uranus—rulers of the 11th house

Positive: Humane, intuitive, unbiased
Negative: Rebellious, suspicious, inefficient
Career: Philosopher, scientist

PISCES —The Fishes, Feb. 19–Mar. 20
    (Governs the feet)
Jupiter, Neptune—rulers of the 12th house

Positive: Compassionate, psychic, sacrificing
Negative: Hypersensitive, melancholic, drifting
Career: Poet, actor, interpreter, comedian

SESSION GUIDE

CHALLENGE 6   ASTROLOGY

A. Personal notes/questions on Challenge 6

B. The challenge

1. Is astrology a fake or a valid science? How do you explain its apparent successes?

2. What kinds of questions does Harvey have that astrology answers? Are these important questions? Do you agree with Harvey that the Bible doesn't answer these questions? Explain.

3. What does dependence on a horoscope do to a person's concept of God's providence?

4. Suppose a Christian who believes that astrology is useless, that it offers nothing of real value, still thinks it provides some harmless fun. Is that OK? Or should Christians avoid astrology altogether? Explain.

C. Response

Which approach do you think would work best in a conversation with a person like Harvey?

1. *Confrontation* approach—Show Harvey that astrology is a fake, that its suppositions are not true to reality.

2. *Need-Nourishment* approach—Talk to Harvey about why he is attracted to astrology. Point out that Christianity already provides the answers, meets his needs, gives him the nourishment he seeks.

3. *Test of Tradition* approach—Show Harvey how astrology has departed from the orthodox Christian faith and its teachings. Show him that he has betrayed the authority (Scripture) he pretends to support.

4. Other?

Pictures of Elijah Muhammad Dominates
Black Muslim Convention Stage

BLACK MUSLIMS

Founding: The Nation of Islam, popularly called the Black Muslims, began in 1929 when W. E. Farad, who claimed to be from Mecca, convinced many Detroit blacks that Islam is the true religion of the black people.

After Farad disappeared in 1934, Elijah (Poole) Muhammad, an early convert, became the new leader. He named Farad "the savior" and established the new headquarters of the movement in Chicago.

In the early sixties Malcolm X, American civil rights leader, became the popular spokesman of the Black Muslim movement. In 1964, however, he broke with the movement to return to a more orthodox Islam and was assassinated a year later.

However, after the death of Elijah Muhammad in 1975, Malcom X's ideas continued to influence the movement. Elijah's son, Wallace D. Muhammad, agreeing with Malcom X's sentiments about a more orthodox Islam, has made sweeping changes in the Muslim organization to that end. He has also changed the group's official name to the "World Community of Islam in the West" or the Bilalians (after Bilal, the first black follower of Mohammad).

Following: There are reputed to be about 70,000 Black Muslims, including the well-known boxer, Muhammad Ali. In recent years the sect has received a good deal of assistance from Arab nations and currently owns a private empire of small businesses.

Faith: The faith as proclaimed by Elijah Muhammad included belief in:
  *one God whose proper name is Allah
  *the Holy Qu'ran
  *the Bible (the truth of which has been misinterpreted)
  *Allah's prophets and the scripture they brought
  *the mental (not physical) resurrection of the dead
  *blacks as the people of God's choice
  *the judgment, which will occur first in America
  *the separation of so-called Negroes and so-called white Americans
  *justice for all
And the belief that:
  *the offer of integration is hypocritical
  *righteous Muslims should not participate in wars
  *Muslim women should be respected and protected
  *Allah appeared in the person of W. Farad, who is the messiah of the Christians and the Mahdi of the Muslims
The faith proclaimed by Wallace Muhammad is closer to orthodox Islam. It rejects the divine status of Farad and the title of the "Messenger of God" given to Elijah Muhammad. It also rejects the doctrine of necessary separation of blacks and whites and has opened the sect to all races.

Setting: An uncrowded coffee house or cafe. Music may be funky or straight, depending on whose turf this is. Two young men, obviously friends, obviously athletes, are seated at a table. Darryl is black and Dave is white, though ordinarily that would not matter.

Dave: C'mon, Darryl, be serious.

Darryl: I *am* serious. I didn't reach this point overnight.

Dave: But what about your folks? Forget *my* church, but what about your own?

Darryl: Part of it my folks won't understand, part of it they will—there's a part of it any black can understand. As for my church, in some ways I think it's even worse than yours. I went to your church three, four, how many times? Each time I was welcomed as "Dave Jacob's black friend," or maybe for some as "the black forward who gets good grades at Central." Remember the Pepsi ad a while ago? They didn't run that just to appeal to a bunch of black folks.

Dave: But you *were* welcomed!

Darryl: Sure I was. Relax. But that doesn't change facts: a black on his own in your church is like a fly in the buttermilk. That's not a very comfortable feeling, but it's something I've come to expect from whites. What's worse is the attitude in my own church.

Dave: I don't get it. The people in your congregation made me feel right at home.

Darryl: Just the point. Black churches are coming at you with the same old Christ—the Christ that died for friendship, peace, and big business. And big business belongs to you, not me. Black Christianity's no different today than it was one hundred years ago—it keeps accommodating itself to the white gospel. I've looked as deep as I can into myself, and I know I've got to go in a different direction.

Dave: But why so radical? Why drop your white friends? Why drop school? And didn't you use

True Christianity has never really been applied to the sphere of black-white relations in this country.

Tom Skinner, *How Black Is the Gospel?*, p. 68

The gospel of Jesus Christ is black in the sense that it does not ask a black man to give up his blackness in order to be a Christian.

Tom Skinner, *How Black Is the Gospel?*, p. 78

to describe the Black Muslims as "the lunatic fringe"? How can you decide to join them? You're a Christian!

Darryl: No, I'm not—though for a long time I thought I was. And I think I can explain my change of heart regarding the lunatic fringe thing. But let me start with dropping school and "white folks."

Dave: It's crazy! You're the first guy from our school to get a Big 10 scholarship and you're giving all that up?

Darryl: Try to see it my way. If I were six inches shorter, or scored under fifteen points a game instead of over, I'd be heading for some school in the deep south.

Dave: You think you're being used?

Darryl: Look—take my word for it—all blacks who fit in anywhere are being used. You give us a few scholarships, a few girls, some discreet blank checks and expect our cooperation. Some of us may take the money and say we're using you right back, but we know it's not true. Once we take the money, we try to be as like you as we can. Ever wonder why we're so uptight about keeping cool? A lot of the time we don't like ourselves as much as we should. I want to avoid all that.

Dave: Okay, forget the school a minute—though I think you're insane—but what about us? Why should we go separate ways? We've been friends for years!

Darryl: You're a great guy, Dave, but you're white as snow. If I were the kid in the Pepsi ad, it'd all go great. He'll be a college star and then a broadcaster or a pro, and he'll have white friends and black friends who think white. That just keeps it all going the way it is. I don't want it to keep going.

Dave: I read James Baldwin, too, Darryl. Lots of us do. We sympathize.

Darryl: But have you read Malcom X? We don't need anymore sympathy. I don't, none of us do.

What I *do* need is the right to control my own future—so that maybe I or my children will be in a position to sympathize with *you* someday.

Dave: Okay, I goofed there. But you can't be serious about the Black Muslims. All that stuff about crazy doctrines, black men sixty trillion years ago, separate states for blacks—you can't be serious about all that.

Darryl: You've got it all wrong—things have changed. A few years ago your description would have been right. The Black Muslims did teach some pretty fantastic accounts of how you "blue-eyed devils" came to be. They did demand a separate state and a lot of other things.

And they were a powerful force in their believers' lives. Kids stayed off dope, men stayed with their families; at least some black people were beginning to see they were God's beautiful creation. They also saw the evils of the white society pretty clearly. Remember, Elijah Mohammad had seen his Baptist preacher father murdered. He knew the white person's heart.

Then came Malcolm X. He was the real spokesman for the Muslims, remember? I doubt that most whites ever understood that all of his violent and daring statements weren't meant to shock the whites. They were intended to stir up blacks, like me, to the sort of anger and pride we needed in order to stand up and say we were worth something. But even before Malcolm X was killed, he was changing direction.

And the Muslims have changed direction too. Check out some recent religious magazines—white ones. You won't find much against the Black Muslims. What you'll read instead is something about how Bilalians are becoming more conservative, true followers of Islam, or how they are supporting the country and seeking some sort of peace between people of all colors.

Dave: Isn't that good?

Darryl: Well, it's the same old story: first we stand up

This past summer, Bilalians sponsored a Fourth of July parade down Michigan Avenue in Chicago. Thousands of them marched, many carrying American flags, others bearing posters proclaiming their new-found patriotism: "America Is Hope," "Races United," "Build One Nation."

James Emerson Whitehurst, "The Mainstreaming of the Black Muslims: Healing the Hate," *Christian Century,* February 27, 1980, p. 229

. . . In one important respect [Wallace Muhammad] differs from his father. He believes that now is the time for Bilalians to enter the mainstream of American life.

James Emerson Whitehurst, "The Mainstreaming of the Black Muslims: Healing the Hate," *Christian Century,* February 27, 1980, p. 229

. . . One of the main lessons in the Old Testament of our Bible is that your race should be kept pure. God made different races and put them in different lands. He was satisfied with pure races so man could keep the races pure and be satisfied.
BIRDS DO NOT MIX.
CHICKENS DO NOT MIX.
A friend had 100 white chickens and 100 reds. All the white chickens go to one side of the house, and all the red chickens go on the other side of the house. You probably feel the same way these chickens did whenever you are with people of a different race. God meant it to be that way.

Printed in a textbook officially recommended for fifth and sixth grades by the White Citizens Council of Mississippi.
(from Charles Silberman, *Crisis in Black and White,* 1964, p. 150)

and say, "We gonna be free!" and then we start joining up again—and you use us the way you want to.

Dave: I don't want to say that's true; but if it is, what are you going to do?

Darryl: Just join the Bilalians. They might not be perfect, but they're the best option I've got. If I'm going to survive I've got to be separate and proud and eager for the fight that's coming.

Dave: But we've always talked peace, you and I.

Darryl: Black people talk peace while we're unemployed; we talk it while we go to jail without fair trials, while we smile for toothpaste ads, while we watch you being sorry for us. I'm sorry—I usually keep it under control, but my anger's there too.

Dave: But what about the Bible? The church? Can you just say you don't believe it? Are you going to deny Christ just to get some of the world's justice?

Darryl: I've thought about that a lot. The only Christ I've seen is in churches which teach so much patience that the people sing hymns while society crumbles around them. When I see white Christians overcoming their racism, when I see black Christians recognizing they've passed the need to forgive—then maybe I'll think Christ is alive and well in the churches. Until then, I've got to seek a truth that tells me how black people are as worthwhile as I know they are.

Dave: Can't you reconsider?

Darryl: I've been considering all my life. Next week I graduate, and it's either the white world or my own. I've talked to the coaches, the counselors, the preachers—you name it—and it's all the same. Fit into the system that kills us. But I've determined to live while I'm alive. And I'd like a few other blacks to live while they're alive too.

Silence. Dave moves his lips to speak but realizes he has nothing to say.

90

FOR FURTHER READING

Lincoln, Eric C. *The Black Muslims in America*. Revised Edition. Boston: Beacon Press, 1973.

> Somewhat dated but offers a thorough history of the Black Muslims.

Skinner, Tom. *How Black Is the Gospel?* Philadelphia: Lippincott, 1970.

> Maintains that what the Bible teaches as being Christianity and what the white culture has made Christianity are two different things. Argues that blacks can demand justice without hatred.

Starkers, M.T. *Confronting Popular Cults.* Nashville: Broadman Press, 1972.

> Features a chapter on the Black Muslims and Elijah (Poole) Muhammad. Includes a section on how to witness to Black Muslims (pp. 71–83).

Whitehurst, James Emerson. "The Mainstreaming of the Black Muslims: Healing the Hate," *Christian Century,* February 27, 1980.

> Traces how a "sect grew up and became a church."

CASSETTE TAPES

Martin, Walter. *Black Muslims.* C-75. Available from the Christian Research Institute, Box 500, San Juan Capistrano, California 92693. Write for current prices and brochure.

Black Muslim Convention, Chicago, 1961

SESSION GUIDE

CHALLENGE 7   BLACK MUSLIM

A. Personal notes/questions on Challenge 7

B. Understanding the challenge

    1. According to Darryl, how have the Black Muslims changed recently? Why is Darryl against the change?

    2. What radical change does Darryl argue for?

C. Response (using the *Offense* approach)

    If you were in Dave's position, what would you say to Darryl?

    1. First admit that some of his accusations about the church and Christianity are true. *(Which ones?)*

1 Black are being use
2. not welcome
3.

2. Show that what offends Darryl about the church is not what Christ intended the church to be. *(How did Christ intend the church to be with regard to race relations? What Scriptures could be mentioned?)*

3. Finally, point out that there are certain necessary and unavoidable differences between Darryl's position and Christianity. *(What is Darryl's position, his answer? What basic difference(s) would we cite between that position and Christianity?)*

Compare your answers and approach with that of Response 7.

Werner Erhard

CHALLENGE 8

EST

Founding: Est stands for "it is" (in Latin) and is an acronym for Erhard Seminars Training, a cult begun by Werner Erhard in 1971. Erhard was born in Philadelphia in 1935 and christened John Paul Rosenberg. At the age of twenty-four he deserted his wife Pat and their four children and headed west with Ellen, the woman who became his second wife.

California introduced Erhard to a mixture of philosophies including Scientology, Mind Dynamics, Zen, Hinduism, encounter therapy, and the teachings of Wittgenstein, Maslow, and Perls. But none of them completely convinced Erhard. Then, as he was driving over the Golden Gate Bridge one day, he had a flash of insight, a conversion: "What is, is, and what was, was, and what isn't, isn't." Convinced that he had the solution to human problems, Erhard organized his first seminar and began teaching est.

Following: Est seminars claim over 200,000 graduates, including such prominent entertainers as John Denver, Yoko Ono, and Joanne Woodward. Graduates are usually fairly affluent whites.

Faith: *The world has no meaning or purpose.
*The human mind imposes artificial meanings and purposes on the world.
*As an individual you are the cause of your own world.
*You can become free (god of your own universe) by choosing to

become the author of your own subjective universe of emotions, sensations, and ideas.

*Other people should be granted space to create their own experiences.

June's Story

I love my big brother as I do myself (like the Bible says) but for the next few months I'm going to leave him alone. I still think he's pretty attractive—his taste in clothes and cars is great—but I'll no longer arrange introductions for the single girls in church. He's not a safe bet. I think he's sort of gone off the deep end.

Mother always said Buddy had a future. In fact, we left Chicago for Phoenix right in the middle of *my* second year as a cheerleader so Buddy could "focus attention," as he would say, "on aspects of solar engineering." I think now Mom wishes she'd stayed in Chicago; at least there Dad was still dropping in a few times each week. Here she's got no one but me, and I'm only home now and then. As soon as Buddy got his degree, he built a huge house outside of Tempe and moved over there. Until a few months ago, just after I started my secretarial job with Aetna, he came by on Sundays for church and a quick lunch. But that's ended too.

It's funny to think he's fallen apart, I guess, because last time I saw him he insisted he'd gotten himself together for the first time. And this is funny too: though I couldn't make sense out of what he was saying, he *did* look happier than usual.

We were in a weird Mexican food place, almost a series of caves, and Buddy was saying these really strange things.

"Me and the church," he said. "You can forget it. Before the seminars, I never realized how much the church was pushing me where I didn't want to go."

"What seminars?" I said.

"Est," he said and smiled. "If you had experienced what I did, you would set your next paycheck aside and enroll. Or I'll advance you the money. It's the one ripoff that's worth buying into."

"Is it anti-Christian?" I asked.

"By no means," he said. "Nor is it anti-Zen, nor anti-Communist, nor anti-anything. Just anti-baloney." He paused, then added, "It showed me how much baloney my church was for me. Pure baloney." He didn't ac-

"Est will teach you that you are all right just as you are. If you are not all right, then you will learn that it's all right to be not all right. All of this can be experienced," the bubbly assistant said, "in sixty hours for a cost of only $250."

John P. Newport, *Christ and the New Consciousness*, p. 106

It takes nearly 70 hours to get most or all of the trainees converted, and that time is filled with a variety of techniques and processes designed to alternately confuse and enlighten the subjects, to develop the authority of the trainer and build his suggestive power over the hapless "assholes."

Mark Brewer, "We're Gonna Tear You Down and Put You Back Together," *Psychology Today*, August 1975, p. 39

Anything you're stuck in, you're the effect of. Man can't reason, he can only have *reason. Most people can't feel, they can only have feelings that get pulled out by certain stimuli. That's the way man reasons—on a stimulus-response basis. When you transcend reason, then you are able to reason. Like, for instance, Einstein transcended reason when he developed the theory of relativity. So he was able to reason.*

Mark Brewer, "We're Gonna Tear You Down and Put You Back Together," *Psychology Today,* August 1975, p. 39

The tension and harassment, along with the trauma many of them suffered at standing openly before a large crowd, produced a number of breakdowns. In each row of 30 or 40 persons who took the stage, there were usually four or five who sobbed piteously or even swooned, completely overcome. Tony usually snapped, "That's just another act." One man hung his head and bawled like a soul in hell. Another vomited.

Mark Brewer, "We're Gonna Tear You Down and Put You Back Together," *Psychology Today,* August 1975, p. 82.

tually say "baloney," but I'm mild by nature and choose not to repeat his more colorful language. I guessed that he'd gotten some of his phrases from the seminars.

"But you made public profession of your faith," I said. "That's more than I've done. I don't really see how you can say these things, Buddy."

He straightened up a bit, looking slightly severe. "Look, all my life I was conned. Do this and you're good. Do this and you're bad. But basically you're bad because there's really no way to be good. The only way is to seek salvation."

"Is that bad?" I asked.

"It is when you consider you are seeking salvation from a part of yourself."

"But the church teaches salvation from sin."

"But whose sin is it? Mine. Part of me. All my life I've been worrying about why I kept on doing things that the church said were sin. Or maybe why I couldn't bring Dad and Mom back together just by wanting it. Or why I didn't work harder for grades."

"But you always got A's."

"That's not the point. The point is that I felt guilty about all the things that were screwed up in my life, and the church taught me the answer was sin and I needed salvation."

"Wasn't that right?" I asked.

"What was right was that a lot of things seemed screwed up in my life. Where the church was wrong was in thinking I could get rid of those things. What I needed was a totally new perspective to learn to accept myself. And I got it."

"You've got to explain it to me more," I said, "because I'm going to have to say something to Mom."

Buddy leaned forward a bit, still calm. I used to get some sort of reaction by mentioning Mom, but not this time.

"You don't explain est; it's something you go through, and you either get it or you don't. The way you get it is your own way, not anyone else's, so there's nothing I can tell you about est. Besides it would spoil it for you if you knew what you were in for. I *can* tell you this: think of a boot camp or something tough like that and you can be sure the est seminars are tougher. But in sixty hours or so they do more for you than a boot camp ever will.''

''If you can't tell me about the seminars,'' I said, ''maybe you could at least tell me how your perspective is changed.''

''I can try, but it's a completely different way of seeing yourself. For instance, the church. I used to try to figure out what it was I was supposed to do—and then get upset when I failed to do it. I never thought about who was in control. Now I know it wasn't me in control, it was the church. I wasn't my own cause, just an effect. And you can't be happy as an effect.''

''I don't understand,'' I said.

''Of course not. You're you and I'm me. I know I'm my own cause and can refuse to be anyone's effect. Your church and Mom and your job are all causing you, determining what you will do. So you're an effect in that sense. Unless by accident you happen to agree with those causes, you're bound to be unhappy. I was.''

''But I'm not unhappy,'' I said. ''I believe I ought to obey the church. And Mom, too, for that matter. And every job has rules.''

''Yes, as long as you agree to them. But you don't see that. For you an *ought* is an *is.* But for me the only *ought* is the *ought* I agree to—that's an *ought* that *is.* It *is* because *I* create it—not you or Mom or the church or anyone else. Your *oughts* can be *is* for you but not for me anymore.''

''But what about things like honor your father and mother? You know Mom likes you to stop in for Sunday lunch.''

''And I'll come sometime. But not because she wants me to. I'll come when pleasing her is something *I* want to do—when I can come as my own cause. Now she'd just want to argue religion. I don't want that, so I won't come. If I went to see her when I didn't want to, how would I be happy?''

''Just by knowing it made her happy—you wouldn't have to argue.''

The Miracle. Then came the miracle. If you accept the nature of your mind, Ted explained with a rising optimism in his voice, and take responsibility for having created all the stimulus-response mechanisms it comprises, then in effect you have freely chosen to do everything you have ever done and to be precisely what you are. In that instant, you become exactly what you always wanted to be.

Mark Brewer, ''We're Gonna Tear You Down and Put You Back Together,'' *Psychology Today,* August 1975, p. 88

RULES ABOUT LIFE
by
Werner Erhard

1. Life has no rules.
2.

"Look, June," he answered, "try to understand. If Mom wants to be happy, she's got to see that everything's all right the way it is. She's got to see that she wanted what she has and that's why she has it. When she understands that, she'll get over thinking I should show up either in her home or in her church. Unless I want to."

"Wait a minute," I said. I guess I was a little angry. "You think she wanted the divorce? You think she likes living alone? You think she wanted you to leave the church?"

"Her problem is she doesn't see how she fits in. Neither do you. Neither did I until I got *it*. Now it all comes together and I see that basically we're all doing what we want to do. When a person begins to grasp that what is *is*, he can forget about what isn't and take control."

"Control of what?"

"Of himself. Each person creates the world he wants and wants the world he creates. It's profoundly simple."

"It escapes me, I'm afraid."

Perhaps I sounded too disgusted. Buddy laid a five dollar bill over the check the waitress had brought and stood up.

"The only way to get it is to try the seminars. There's a guest seminar next week in Tempe. I could bring you if you'd like."

I told him I'd think about it. And I am. But like I said, I think I'll leave him alone for a while. I keep feeling there's some questions I'd like to ask him, but I'm not sure what they are.

FOR FURTHER READING

Brewer, Mark. "We're Gonna Tear You Down and Put You Back Together," *Psychology Today,* August 1975.

> In a thorough article, a "stubborn journalist" reports his experience with est and with the super-salesman who invented it out of psycho-techniques, Eastern and Western. When you know you're a mechanical "anus," you've "got it."

Hoekema, David. "The Hunger Project: You Can't Eat Words," *Christian Century,* May 2, 1979.

> Points out how an est hunger project does not provide food for the hungry but rather spends its money on conferences, communications, and so on.

Newport, John P. *Christ and the New Consciousness.* Nashville: Broadman Press, 1978.

> Discusses in a short chapter the history of est, its teachings, and its methods. Offers a critique from a secular and theological point of view. The author attended an est seminar.

Weldon, John. *The Frightening World of Est.*

> A new book on est available from Beta Book Co., 10857 Valiente Ct., San Diego, California. Cost: $4.95, plus 75¢ postage (California residents add 30¢ sales tax).

CASSETTE TAPES

Martin, Walter. *The New Cults: Est.* C-79. Available from the Christian Research Institute, Box 500, San Juan Capistrano, California 92693. Write for current prices and brochure.

Werner Erhard

SESSION GUIDE

CHALLENGE 8   EST

A. Personal notes/questions on Challenge 8

To prepare for next week's class session on est, please think about and answer these questions:

—What does est teach about the self? Underline key lines in Challenge 8.

It has no meaning or purpose. Self is all important.

—What does Christianity, by contrast, teach about the self? Check such passages as Matthew 6:33, 16:24–25, 22:36–40; Romans 12:1–2; Ephesians 2:8; and Heidelberg Catechism Q & A 1.

Deny yourself and take up your cross and follow Jesus. Love the Lord your God with all your heart. Present your bodies as a living sacrifice to the Lord.

B. Challenge and response

How should June attempt to convince her brother to return to the Christian faith? What should she tell him?

Est believers like Buddy can be approached in various ways by Christians. At the back of your textbook, five apologetic approaches are described. With the others in your group, work on developing *one* of these approaches. Outline what you would say to Buddy using that particular approach.

Guide questions to consider when outlining your approach are included below.

COMMON GROUND APPROACH

What partial truths does Buddy express, truths we can agree with? How can we build on these truths to show Buddy the full, Christian truth? What *is* the full, Christian truth?

CONFRONTATION APPROACH

How might est's beliefs about the self prove very uncomfortable if pushed to their logical conclusions? What "hard" questions might we ask Buddy to bring out these uncomfortable conclusions?

NEED-NOURISHMENT APPROACH

What are Buddy's deepest needs? Does est really satisfy those needs? Can Christianity do a better job of meeting those needs? How?

OFFENSE APPROACH

What mistaken ideas does Buddy have about the church? How would we correct these ideas? What clear differences between est and Christianity would we finally have to stress?

TEST OF TRADITION APPROACH

Buddy claims that est is not anti-Christian. Show him—from the Bible and confessions—that est does in fact depart from traditional, orthodox Christian teachings.

Bibliography

"Astrology: Fad and Phenomenon." *Time,* 21 March 1969, pp. 48 and 54.

Back to Godhead, vol. 6, no. 11. Los Angeles: Bhaktivedanta Book Trust.

Brewer, Mark. "We're Gonna Tear You Down and Put You Back Together." *Psychology Today,* August 1975, p. 39.

Cunningham, Sister Agnes. "A Critique of the Theology of the Unification Church as Set Forth in 'Divine Principle.'" *Occasional Bulletin,* July 1977, pp. 18–23.

Déchanet, Jean Marie. *Christian Yoga.* London: Burns & Oates, 1960.

Elam, Tom. "Who Is Maharishi Mahesh Yogi?" *Phi Delta Kappan,* December 1972, p. 237.

Ellwood, R. *Religious and Spiritual Groups in Modern America.* Englewood Cliffs, N.J.: Prentice-Hall, 1973.

Gillespie, Tom. "To the Moon and Back...An Interview with an Ex-Moonie." *Psychiatric Nursing,* March–April 1980, pp. 6–10.

Guinness, Os. "The East, No Exit." *Eternity,* December 1973, pp. 26–30.

Jornstad, James B. and Johnson, Shildes. *Stars, Signs, and Salvation in the Age of Aquarius.* Minneapolis, Minn.: Dimension Books, 1971.

Keeler, Scott. "A California Teenager Goes Underground to Investigate Life among the Moonies." *People,* 24 July 1978, pp. 20–7.

Landmarks, yr. 1, vol. III, no. 5. "Age of Aquarius." Grand Rapids, Mich.: Board of Publications of the Christian Reformed Church, 1980.

Levine, Paul H. "Transcendental Meditation and Science of Creative Intelligence." *Phi Delta Kappan,* December 1972, pp. 231–5.

Maust, John. "The Moonies Cross Wits with Cult-watching Critics." *Christianity Today,* 20 July 1979, pp. 38–40.

McBeth, Leon. *Strange New Religions.* Nashville: Broadman Press, 1977.

Meyer, Ray. *Baha'i, Follower of the Light.* Wilmette, Ill.: Baha'i Publishing Trust, 1972.

Newport, J. P. *Christ and the New Consciousness.* Nashville: Broadman Press, 1978.

Oates, Robert. *Celebrating the Dawn.* New York: Putnam, 1976.

Rice, Berkeley. "Honor Thy Father." *Psychology Today,* January 1976, pp. 36–47.

Riley, J. C. "Astrological Research Bulletin." *Grand Rapids Press,* 21 August 1975.

Russell, Peter. *The TM Technique, An Introduction to Transcendental Meditation on the Teachings of Maharishi Mahesh Yogi.* Boston: Routledge and K. Paul, 1976.

Sage, Wayne. "The War on the Cults." *Human Behavior,* October 1976, pp. 40–9.

Schaff, Philip, ed. *A Select Library of the Nicene and Post-Nicene Fathers of the Christian Church,* vol. XIV. Grand Rapids, Mich.: Wm. B. Eerdmans Pub. Co., 1956.

Scientology: A World Religion Emerges in the Space Age. Hollywood, Calif.: Church of Scientology Information Service, Department of Archives, 1974.

Silberman, Charles. *Crisis in Black and White.* New York: Random House, 1964.

Skinner, Tom. *How Black Is the Gospel?* Philadelphia: Lippincott, 1970.

Slaughter, Cynthia. "To Another Plane—and Back." *Time,* 14 June 1976, p. 50.

Starkes, M. Thomas. *Today's World Religions.* New Orleans: Insight Press, 1978.

Wallis, Roy. *Sectarianism.* New York: Wiley, 1975.

Whitehurst, James E. "The Mainstreaming of the Black Muslims: Healing the Hate." *Christian Century,* 27 February 1980, p. 229.

FIVE APOLOGETIC APPROACHES

The chart below outlines five basic ways to defend your faith. Remember that in actual practice, emphasizing the love of God and witnessing with your life are at least as important as using any of these approaches. But knowing about the approaches will give you a starting point, a way to organize your own thinking and a plan to present your faith to others.

Your Reasons teacher will give you additional information on any of these approaches.

	ADVANTAGES	DISADVANTAGES
COMMON GROUND — Begins with a friendly discussion of what the two faiths have in common. Then attempts to show that what the other faith believes is only partially true and that the Christian faith provides a deeper, more complete truth, a better perspective on the world, a better answer to the questions and problems.	Keeps the discussion conversational, low-key, reasonable.	Can be seen by opponent as compromising; may make your faith seem weak to other person.
CONFRONTATION — Directly attacks (confronts) the contrasting faith, trying to show that its beliefs are either unrealistic or logically inconsistent and that, if pushed to their logical conclusions, these beliefs will be untenable and/or unlivable. Finally, may present the Christian system as the only one that is realistic and consistent.	Other person knows clearly where you stand. No waffling. Also appeals to those who value logic, consistency.	May antagonize the other person, not convince him, especially if he is so committed to his faith that he won't even discuss its flaws.

Begins by probing what deep, inner needs are met by the contrasting faith, needs such as the desire for security, for self-esteem, for belonging, for understanding and beauty. Then shows that Christianity and Christ provide more than enough nourishment to live meaningfully, more than any other faith or belief system.

Addresses the life experiences of a person. Appeals to deep psychological and spiritual needs.

May not be effective with those whose needs were not met in the past by the Christian church, and whose needs are apparently now fully satisfied within the cult or sect.

OFFENSE

Begins by trying to remove unnecessary offenses (objections, obstacles) the contrasting faith raises against Christianity. Accomplished by correcting misunderstandings or misrepresentations of Christianity. Finally attempts to bring out the *real* differences between Christianity and the contrasting faith, making what is the necessary and unavoidable offense unmistakably clear.

Helpful when a person obviously has wrong notions about Christianity. Helpful for exposing real, important differences.

Could be ineffective if the other person's wrong notions about Christianity are based on her personal experience with the church and Christians.

TEST OF TRADITION

Simply shows that those who hold other positions have departed from the original orthodox/Christian faith. They have failed the test of tradition and have betrayed the authority they pretend to recognize (the Bible or the church or Christ).

Especially helpful for sects with Christian roots. Encourages genuine discussion of authorities (Bible, church, Christ) held in common.

Sects and cults often adhere rigidly to their interpretation of Scripture. Also, requires thorough knowledge of Scripture and traditional orthodox beliefs.

Responses
to the
challenges
are to be
kept in the
attached
envelope. ➡

Response 8
EST

Does June stand a chance of reaching Buddy? Only if she's prepared for a struggle. Buddy has been "converted" to est, and recent converts are usually strongly committed to their new beliefs. Before June approaches her brother again, she better do her homework; it's vital that she read enough to understand the system she's arguing against.

Est seminars are *designed* to produce a conversion. Participants are subjected to long sessions of verbal abuse in uncomfortable surroundings. They are "browbeaten" with skillfully employed scorn and ridicule until they are ready to discard all previous beliefs. Then they are informed that since they can't be anything other than what they are—since nothing is real except the products of their own minds—they can accept themselves as already being perfectly what they wanted to be. They can now take total control.

It may be hard for June to believe Buddy has swallowed this line, but each year thousands do. And there is sociological evidence to suggest that est does open many "estian's" minds to what they see as a more full and free participation in life than they had previously experienced.

Perhaps one area June may try to explore in a future conversation with Buddy is why he accepts est's description of himself as true and rejects his church's message as false. The irony is that, as he relates it, he sees the same message in the initial teachings of both est and Christianity. "What was right was that a lot of things seemed screwed up in my life." Buddy correctly recognizes that the teachings of the Christian church *do* convict a person of her own sin or "badness"; he's not accurate when he sums up the rest of the church's message as "seek salvation."

Somehow, through either the church's errors or his own, Buddy has missed a real point. In terms of Christianity one doesn't seek salvation so much as accept it. It is given. In a very real sense, one simply "gets it." Buddy says, "Where the church was wrong was in thinking I could get rid of those things." But the true focus of the church must be on the fact that the question of personal guilt has been settled in the believer's favor. In that sense—and it seems that this is what Buddy fails to see—the Christian *is* rid of the things that mess up his or her life.

Why didn't Buddy experience the freedom from guilt and failure that Christianity offers? This may be an area for June and Buddy to discuss.

A second question to explore is why Buddy resents being "conned" by the church and yet accepts est as "the only ripoff that's worth buying into." In a way est boldly presents itself as a ripoff. One signs up and pays to find out what is real. In return est takes away all of what a person has known as created reality, leaving her with only the self to rely on. A lot has been "ripped off."

Buddy does not see it this way. The self alone may have been precisely what he wanted. That might explain why he was not happy with the message of Christianity. At the bottom line Christianity demands that the self be yielded through Christ to God. Thus "I belong to *me*" and "I control *myself*" are positions the Christian cannot honestly assume.

Est promotes a radically different experience, designed to lead to the conviction that "I am my own master" and "I may do as I please." The Christian may see this position as an open invitation to trouble and despair; yet many followers of est find in it liberation from systems of thought or belief which they found oppressive.

If Buddy has adopted est out of a desire for personal freedom, June has at least two tasks to accomplish. She must not only reveal to Buddy the personal freedom found in Christianity but also encourage him to question whether est is offering real freedom or a sophisticated type of personal bondage.

One way for June to approach this task is to help Buddy probe est's responses to the presence of what Christians call *sin* in the world. For example, evidence suggests that est does not attract and does not *want* to attract the poor. Poverty is not a concern of est. Though est has a hunger project in operation, it is designed only to help individuals decide for themselves whether it would please them personally to help end world hunger. No evidence suggests that the money est collects for world hunger is used to purchase or distribute food. After all, est teaches that one solves a problem merely by making people aware of their personally chosen role in that problem. If you make people aware that they don't want other people to be hungry, they will then solve the problem of other people's hunger.

June can also explore how est handles the question of personal evil when manifested on a grand scale. What about Hitler? What about murderers and oppressive dictators and horribly cruel parents? Can one say each is perfect the way he or she is, having created their own illusions? Est would and must say that—although one could predict that Buddy will not want to push est to such far-reaching conclusions.

Yet if a system of belief and action is to be evaluated, these are the conclusions one must push toward. June must show Buddy that Christianity can and does draw conclusions about such cases, no matter how extreme. It can convict, it can oppose, it can forgive and present God's offer of redemption. And it can and must separate the sinner from the sin. Thus it is able to include in its area of concern the poorest peasant and the richest king.

It may take time but, if June has the patience to pursue Buddy without anger, Buddy may begin to see that her questions about their mother demand more complicated answers than est can give. Those questions reflect a small part of the wrongdoing in this world that cannot be simplified by assigning each individual total control over self.

June must get Buddy to see that a world in which each person creates her own reality is an insane world. Our lives have meaning not because we make the meaning, but because it exists independently from us, proceeding from the Creator of the universe, God, "in whom we live and move and have our being." This is the freedom June must help Buddy find.

Response 7

BLACK MUSLIMS

What will we Christians say to Darryl? What we say may depend great-
ly on ourselves and on the background of experience out of which we
speak.

Some of us are white Christians with little or no significant understanding of the black culture as it is expressed in North America.

Some of us are black Christians with understanding of but little sympathy for the radical position Darryl is about to take.

Some of us, black or white Christians, may have enough experience or
interaction with each other's culture to realize that easy answers are not
within our grasp.

Few if any among sensitive Christians will assert that they know an
easy answer.

And yet the answer is there—though it is not easy. Before we look at
the answer, however, let's examine some of Darryl's challenges to the
church and to the society.

"A black on his own in your church. . . ." Darryl sees that few white
churches can accept black members with the sort of calm and open

friendship which confirms that the black person is both welcome and not out-of-place. We who are white must learn to admit this: a black visitor from Africa wearing impressive robes gets our attention and our respect as a celebrity, but a black visitor from down the street a ways is a surprise and not always a pleasant one.

Darryl faults his own church for "accommodating itself to the white gospel." We who are black must grant that black Christianity has a long tradition of focusing on the salvation that is coming, on the patience to endure, on a belief that the right will overcome the wrong "someday." We may point out that in a world of white power and control that often seemed—and sometimes still seems—absolute, there was little choice for black Christianity to grow in any other direction. But to explain a problem hardly ever explains it away.

Thus our first step, black or white, in responding to Darryl's charges against the church is to plead guilty. If we can't do that we will fail, and Darryl must truly go his own way.

Darryl's second charge is against white society as a whole; he focuses on the athletic world, but his point is that white society has developed, perhaps unconsciously, a system of rewarding the black person with acceptance and honor only when the person is exceptionally useful to that white society.

Again: score a point for Darryl. Black or white, no Christian willing to continue the discussion can avoid the frank admission that North American society has racism worked deeply into its heart. Perhaps we may argue that if North America could be understood, it could be forgiven. But forgiving a nation or two for causing a problem will not make the problem disappear. So we accept Darryl's second premise: the white-dominated society and church exhibit racist practices in countless ways.

At this point one may ask: if we concede all of Darryl's points, what will we defend? And here is where we meet the answer that is not easy. We must defend nothing, white or black alike, and instead examine the alternatives left us after we've agreed that Darryl, not Dave, sees the problem correctly. If we do so, we must make at least two considerations.

First, for white or black Christians to leave things as they are is not acceptable. A church that preaches a Christ who came that we might have life "more abundantly" may not allow racism to endure in any form. Nor may it push the consideration of achieving the abundant life to some distant future: "the kingdom of God is among you" Christ said, and it must show.

Second, Christians, once they recognize the need for radical change, must urge each other and the outsider to consider carefully the two possible directions change in race relations can take.

Darryl's direction is an attempt to gain dignity for black people by increasing the separation between black and white. The Christian must consider this the wrong direction. In a loving manner the Christian must point out that to justify this direction one must not only abandon Christianity but also the entire concept of a God who cares for all of humanity. To separate people from each other, one must develop separate gods for each separate group.

Let us pray that Darryl might accept this criticism. If he were able to, he might listen to Dave as he proposed a more helpful direction. That direction is toward truly ending the injustice, the usury, and all other forms of racism—not so much because we want to but because recognition of the very person of Christ demands it.

Dave may be able to remind Darryl that no matter what the church in any local time or place may look like, it has received its pattern from the Christ it professes to worship. He can point out that Christ told the parable of the good Samaritan—an attack on racism with divine sanction. He spoke to the woman at the well. He recruited disciples who, in his name, broke down distinctions between Jew and Greek.

Dave must make clear to Darryl that it is *that* Christ he serves. He must be willing to demonstrate with his own life that that Christ *is* alive and well. If he can do that, Darryl may see that what he truly seeks may be found more fully within the church than without.

But if Dave cannot do this, he had better keep quiet; very likely there is nothing more to say.

 ARIES—The Ram, Mar. 21–Apr. 19
(Governs the head)
Mars, Pluto—rulers of the 1st house

Positive: Enterprising, incisive, spontaneous
Negative: Impatient, impetuous
Career: Pioneer, architect, soldier

Response 6
ASTROLOGY

Harvey Willard has dared to ask some important questions. If we have anything to say to him, it may be best to begin by assuring him that we share an interest in his questions.

According to Harvey he moved toward astrology partly out of personal frustration: he was looking for answers and his Scripture-quoting friends couldn't agree on what the correct answers were.

We don't know what Harvey's question was—he mentions something about getting married—but each of us can easily substitute a dozen of our own *little* questions. For Harvey, and most likely for us, *big questions* consider the universe and its control. *Little questions* concern the ins and outs of how you and I survive as minute but yet important parts of that universe. At least important to ourselves.

And we know Harvey is right about the importance of those little questions. We live with them all the time; and much of our future success or failure does depend on the answers we give them: Should I marry? Should I marry *him*? Should I marry him *now*?

Harvey is wrong, however, when he states that the Bible isn't concerned with those questions. True, as he says, the Bible does not try to answer those questions. But it is precisely because the Bible *is* concerned with them that it does *not* answer them. The Bible provides what we need instead of answers.

The possible answer to many of these questions is contained in what we might consider the Bible's *one big answer to one big question.* Let's state the question as "What is the meaning of it all?" and put everything we can think of into the word *it.* A good statement of the Bible's one big answer (though not the only statement of it) is: "The world we know, corrupted by sin, is a creation of a loving God, who through Christ has redeemed it from its sin, is working out that redemption in and through the creatures in that world, and will finally unite all things in himself."

How does this answer relate to those *little questions*? The practice of seeking answers to life's questions by resorting to a method or technique not rooted in God's redemptive love deprives the Christian of important elements of faith and trust. Perhaps we can state it this way for Harvey: the Christian life is not one of foolish risk-taking; but it *is* one of joyfully taking the risks one must take in order to live by faith.

Put it another way. My horoscope may tell me not to marry on Monday. The Bible won't give me that sort of advice. What the Bible will do, however, is open my eyes to see the context of faith and obedience within which I may be assured of God's desire to bring good to me out of either my single or married state. In that context I may make sensible use of my friends' advice, my own intuition, economic data—the list can go on and on, but all of these exist in a God-governed world. And at some point I make a response to all this in Christian faith. I make a decision. I may risk being wrong, but I don't risk the loss of God's redeeming presence.

To look for guidance from the horoscope is to miss the exciting message of God's love in Christ and the freedom we have because of that love. It is as if we refuse to trust God to govern things that are beyond our grasp and refuse to accept personal responsibility for our lives: "I am not responsible for what I do because it was all determined by something in the universe which didn't particularly have me in mind." Such thinking is not consistent with the Christian's understanding of God's revelation. It puts a set of planets between the Christian and her loving Lord.

Harvey is asking another good question when he desires to know himself better. He says astrology has helped "me understand myself a little more than I did before."

No one can criticize Harvey's desire for more understanding of himself and his daily experiences. But we must ask whether a knowledge of self based on a doubtful view of the universe can be considered real knowledge. Astrology has been effectively discredited time and again. It ought by now to be thoroughly undermined. Those areas of astrological investigation which seem to contain what we can assent to as truth have long ago been assigned to other more trustworthy disciplines such as astronomy and physics. Even a cursory investigation will lead a skeptic to the realization that among the various cultures of the world the horoscope functions as only one of many devices used to forecast the future or give advice to the uncertain person.

Harvey may reply that because astrology is just one of these many devices for forecasting it is simply a harmless toy, useful only because the astrologist is using his or her common sense in dispensing advice based on the interpetation of one horoscope. If it's only a toy, why all the fuss?

First, if it is only a toy, its immense popularity suggests that it is a very important toy. But it is *not* a toy. It is a highly suspect system of analysis that leads people away from true reliance on their Creator.

Harvey's questions are good ones, but they deserve better answers than astrology can give. The answers must involve the freedom from fear of the future that can be found only when one's faith and hope is secure in the God who is our only comfort in life and death. Astrology simply does not lead us to that God.

"I have no patience with such stuff. . . . You should persuade me that astrology is a true science! I was a monk, and grieved my father; I caught the Pope by his hair, and he caught me by mine; I married a runaway nun, and begat children with her. Who saw that in the stars? Who foretold that? Astronomy is very good, astrology is humbug."

Martin Luther
(James B. Jornstad and Shildes Johnson, *Stars, Signs, and Salvation in the Age of Aquarius*, p. 86)

What do you understand by the providence of God?

Providence is the almighty and ever present power of God by which he upholds, as with his hand, heaven and earth and all creatures, and so rules them that leaf and blade, rain and drought, fruitful and lean years, food and drink, health and sickness, prosperity and poverty—all things, in fact, come to us not by chance but from his fatherly hand.

Heidelberg Catechism Q & A 27

Reasons I, ©1981, Board of Publications of the Christian Reformed Church, 2850 Kalamazoo Ave. SE, Grand Rapids, MI 49560

Response 5

HARE KRISHNA

People who have met followers of Hare Krishna in shopping malls, airports, or on street corners know that what Mike Greer says about his appearance is true. And they also know that "those crazy robes and shaved heads" create a problem: we may be inclined to reject the devotee of Krishna simply because superficial differences in clothes and behavior are so striking.

Yet those very differences in appearance and lifestyle spring from concerns the Christian and the Krishna devotee share. Among those concerns are the desire for salvation, the rejection of materialism, and the acceptance of an ultimate authority. On these matters we can find common ground to meet and talk with Mike Greer and his fellow devotees—a cult described by one writer as "the ultimate dropouts" from American society.

The Desire for Salvation. Like the Krishna devotee, the Christian often recognizes his life on this earth as shabby and inadequate. Convinced that depths of perception and heights of exaltation *do* exist and *ought* to be a part of one's experience, the Christian appreciates the attempt a person may make to get beyond the ordinariness of life.

The Christian also shares with the follower of Krishna the conviction that the drug scene offers only unsatisfactory solutions. For the Christian, the most fully realized life is that lived in submission to her Lord. Submission to Jesus Christ, however, is very different from submission to Krishna and leads to a fundamentally different concept of salvation.

Submission to Krishna through His Divine Grace Swami Prabhupada involves one in an attempt to deny the value of the body and the material world. A person learns to despise her personal self, her sexual nature, and her physical surroundings. This involves the Krishna devotee in an intricate "legal system," whereby salvation is attained through the debasement of self.

For the Christian, salvation is a freely given gift which, when accepted, leads a person to a more complete expression of individuality. Legal systems are out because the Christian is learning a new freedom in obedience to Christ. That freedom from "legal systems" is a concept which must be lovingly conveyed to the Krishna devotee.

Rejection of Materialism is a second area where the Christian and the Krishna devotee should touch base. When the world of money and things begin to separate the Christian from his God and from his fellow humans, that world is viewed as an enemy trying to destroy the Christian's inner peace. The devotee of Krishna will very likely agree that the material world is an enemy; one might explore with her the way to deal with this enemy.

The Hare Krishna movement concentrates on training the devotee to escape from the material world by viewing it as an illusion—unreal except as a way back to awareness of God. Christianity, viewing the world as created by and distinct from God, promotes an attitude of accepting the material creation as another of God's gifts which can be fully enjoyed only when used as God intends.

God's Authority is a third area of concern to both the Christian and the Krishna devotee. Here the Christian must seek to explore how the Lordship of Jesus Christ and the authority of the Bible differ from the interpretation of the Vedic scriptures by Swami Prabhupada. An interesting contrast can be seen in the way historic Christianity has employed councils to discern the Holy Spirit's leading in the interpretation of Scripture rather than put its faith in the interpretation of any one person.

By meeting the Krishna devotee "where she's at" and not being put off by her "strangeness," the Christian may be able to demonstrate to the devotee that, by following His Divine Grace, she is following a road not to a new freedom from her old self, but to a new bondage in which she must struggle to subdue that self by an extremely legalistic system. And if the Christian can provide ex-Hare Krishna converts with a social and religious community that is willing to make a home for them, he may be justified in persuading the devotee to seek true freedom in Jesus Christ.

How are you right with God?

Only by true faith in Jesus Christ.

    Even though my conscience accuses me
        of having grievously sinned against all God's
        commandments
        and of never having kept any of them,
    and even though I am still inclined toward all evil,
    nevertheless,
        without my deserving it at all,
        out of sheer grace,
    God grants and credits to me
    the perfect satisfaction, righteousness, and holiness of Christ,
        as if I had never sinned nor been a sinner,
        as if I had been as perfectly obedient
            as Christ was obedient for me.

All I need to do
is to accept this gift of God with a believing heart.

Heidelberg Catechism Q & A 60

If anyone asserts the fabulous pre-existence of souls, and shall assert the monstrous restoration which follows from it; let him be anathema (Anathema I).

Statement from the Fifth Ecumenical Council (A.D. 553). Philip Shaff, *A Select Library of the Nicene and Post-Nicene Fathers of the Christian Church*, Vol. XIV, pp. 318–9

It is only the Christian faith—with a God who is, with an Incarnation that is earthy and historical, with a salvation that is at cross-purposes with human nature, with a resurrection that blasts apart the finality of death—that is able to provide an alternative to the dust of death settling down over both East and West.

Os Guinness, "The Dust of Death," *Eternity*, December 1973, p. 30

Do you want to go shopping with me if my mother take us to G.R.

Response 4
THE CHURCH OF SCIENTOLOGY

1012 Walnut Street
Vancouver, British Columbia
Wednesday, December 2

Alan Miller
2434 Menominee Drive
Portland, Oregon

Dear Alan,

It was great to get your letter, though I'm really confused about my sister's comments; I had no idea you were out of school at all! Kind of funny, 'cause it still seems as if we're always doing opposite things. I hitchhiked my way through Alberta and British Columbia, even worked illegally parttime on the railroad, and really thought about never settling down at all—until I met Sue in Vancouver. A bum can't afford to think of marriage, which is why I'm in dental school (actually predental, but I'm doing well). Some of your scholarship must have accidentally rubbed off on me.

So now you're out of school and I'm in. And I gather you're still unattached, while Sue and I are planning how to finance marriage and maybe a family. And I've become more and more convinced of the truths of Christianity, while you seem to have headed in a different direction there too.

I *do* remember those "heavy talks." They were a lot heavier for me than you because I was never the intellectual you were. I just slogged through to get the grade, and those talks often helped me do that. But I never felt I was able to hold my own when you really got going.

So all I could do when you mentioned Scientology was look it up in magazines and a few books to see what I could find. So far what I have found disturbs me a lot. Be patient with me because I have more questions than answers at the moment.

One of the first questions I raise is about the reputation of this L. Ron Hubbard. Your portrayal of him is very positive, but some pretty good sources raise a lot of questions. For instance, one of his associates in the world of science fiction claims that long before Hubbard promoted his teachings of Scientology, he had said that writing was a pretty poor way to try to get rich—and that if a person really wanted to make it big financially, he should start a new religion.

If that were the only thing, I still wouldn't ask too many questions, but there's more. Hubbard claims several questionable degrees. One school he claimed to graduate from only recorded him as dropping out after a very poor performance. Nothing against dropping out, you understand, but it seems as if some serious misrepresentation has been going on. If Hubbard has not been completely honest in the past, why should I trust him now?

Another area that I found worth investigating was the history of the emergence of Scientology as a religion. The early stages, I'm sure you already know, were centered around the bestselling book *Dianetics* which presented Scientology minus its doctrines about the soul and reincarnations. At first Hubbard's theories were promoted as a sort of science or medical knowledge being made available to the public. But when the system was attacked by the scientists and others in court, Hubbard began proclaiming his theories were a religion.

Which makes me wonder if possibly the change to religious status was introduced just to sell the product. If Hubbard was not being perfectly honest and was interested in selling something, he might be accused of creating a religion just because he could not be so easily attacked by the courts. I must sound terribly suspicious of him, but these are things I'm really thinking and we've never hid our thoughts from each other before. I'm afraid this Hubbard is a charlatan!

Another thing is the way Scientology raises support. They call it, I believe, fixed donations. But critics point out that often to reach "Clear," a person will spend more than five thousand dollars. And to reach the many levels of operating Thetan costs even more money. What sort of religion, I wonder, exacts large amounts of money from parishioners who wish to become more pure or holy, or who wish to reach higher states of experience?

Early critics attacked *Dianetics* as dangerous because it might lead the person who needed professional psychological help or counseling to try a do-it-yourself method that would prove more harmful than helpful. I notice that Scientology's literature now states quite clearly that those who need medical help or those who are judged mentally ill are not permitted to become members. That raises other questions: What sort of faith deliberately excludes the truly needy in favor of those who already are healthy and who can pay? What sort of religion claims its goal is "to make the able more able"?

Perhaps it's not fair to judge Scientology by listening to its critics— though the fact that they are so numerous makes me think there must be some substance to their charges. I *did* go through some of Scientology's own literature, and I found myself confused. The language is scientific and modern, all right, but it doesn't appear very clear to me. In fact, some of the basic statements of the church sound like total jargon!

> *Life is Basically Static.* Definition: *A Life Static* has no mass, no motion, no wavelength, no location in space or time. It has the ability to postulate and to perceive.

Maybe this is profound, or maybe it's just nonsense. But I find myself confused by it rather than impressed. I compared it in my mind to the first part of the Apostles' Creed:

I believe in God the Father, Almighty, maker of Heaven and Earth, and in Jesus Christ, his only begotten Son, our Lord. . . .

When I look at these two statements, Alan, I think first that the Scientology statement is attempting to reduce religious mysteries to a definition a believer could understand logically or scientifically. That would be very fine if I could actually understand it. But I can't. The Apostles' Creed does not presume to explain anything regarding the mystery or majesty of God. It asserts that mystery and majesty as a revelation to be accepted by faith.

The second thing I notice about these statements and the others I have examined is that while Christianity is always concerned about God and his dealings with humans and our obligation to be related to God through faith, God seems to disappear from the picture in Scientology. Everything is centered around what a person can do for himself. I remain convinced at this point that whenever I try to do things by and for myself, I end up more frustrated than before. I think the picture the Bible presents of humanity's dependence on God is pretty accurate.

These are a few of the questions I have. I haven't mentioned the engrams and the reincarnation ideas because they really sound like science fiction to me. In fact that's what I suggest for your next letter. If you can go dispassionately (yes, I remember that word, Alan!) through the articles I'm sending you and then defend Mr. Hubbard against the charge that he has constructed a giant ripoff by using science fiction and scientific jargon to "sell" those who want something new and exciting and who aren't too fussy about truth, we might have another heavy talk on our hands.

Sincerely,
Sam

Reasons I, ©1981, Board of Publications of the Christian Reformed Church, 2850 Kalamazoo Ave. SE, Grand Rapids, MI 49560

DIVINE REVELATORS

GOD

Response 3
BAHA'I—THE CHILDREN OF LIGHT

Instructor's Comments: Comparative Religions 103

I want to take extra time to reply to your essay as well as to grade it, Eleanor. You apologized for writing a less-than-objective essay. The important thing is that you recognized what you were doing. I'll look for the objective report in the next assignment, but in a way I must say I prefer the paper you've written to many of the objective kind. I say this because it's so easy to see that your heart is in what you write.

You have studied the historical background of Baha'i, and you grew up aware of the Islamic background which gave rise to this new faith. So though I'm supposed to be teaching from an historical point of view, I'll also take some liberties and try to reply to some of your particular concerns.

Let me start with *how three religions can claim to be the only true one.* Actually, there are many religions that claim to have the only correct view of humanity and the universe. We've not yet touched on the great religions of the East in this course, but they can and do lay claim to being universal religions too. They tend to teach that the only reality is God himself, that the material world is illusory, of little worth, or even evil in itself. In their view human beings must learn to escape their bodies and the rest of the material world. I would prefer to group Judaism, Christianity, and Islam together as standing opposed to these Eastern religions, since all three assert that the material world is real and of worth, and that its real worth is best expressed in relation to the God who created and still loves that world.

If you can accept that definition, you can see that it may be helpful to think of these three religions as three aspects of that view of humanity, the material world, and God. One could make a good case for treating Judaism as the prophetic stage which sets the scene for Christianity, and one could describe Islam as a modification (some would say imitation) of Christianity—a Christianity altered to make it particularly acceptable to the Arabic world.

As a Christian, the event that brings these "aspects" into sharp focus is the death and resurrection of Jesus Christ. Here the whole religious world is confronted with two ideas: the once-for-all redemption of creation through Christ, and the insistence on the importance of the body—the physical side of creation—purified and renewed through that redemption.

It is with and through the person of Christ that the Christian faces the entire collection of competing religions, and I believe Baha'i is susceptible to criticism at this point. I'll get back to that in a few paragraphs.

If I've understood your paper correctly, you are attracted to Baha'i chiefly because it proclaims as a new gospel, especially appropriate to today, truths which you agree with and do not see as clearly evident in other faiths.

You are certainly right when you deplore the racism, or the theological infighting, or the denial of human rights to a particular group or sex in our churches. I've seen it too and I too have been dismayed. But I don't think this defines the church. Christ Jesus defines the church, and he allows no room for such practices. He accepted Samaritans, he accepted women, and he prayed that his disciples would avoid controversy and be united as a proof of the truth of his witness.

What happened? Obviously the Christian church has let Christ down. The reason? As Christ was well aware, the temptation to seek our own ends apart from God can be seen in the church as well as outside it. Sin is just as real as any other part of reality. My point is that when you look at what the Christian church stands for, you see the truths you are looking for. But when you look at Christians as they live, you see the effects of sin that Christ was so aware of.

In the presentations of Baha'i I have seen, the emphasis is on what they stand for—and there I have no particular quarrel with them. But nowhere in the Baha'i faith do I find a realistic assessment of human bondage to sin; nor do I find a focus on how one escapes that very real bondage.

Or put it this way: Baha'i proclaims a set of high ideals and an organization for people who follow those ideals. Christianity proclaims the same high ideals, but recognizes that each Christian is involved in a confrontation between those ideals and the very real presence of sin in one's life.

Which brings us back again to Jesus Christ, the Christian's only hope. It is precisely through his life, death, resurrection, and continuing presence that the church asserts the victory of each believer over the power of sin. This is not the traditional role of a prophet. It is the role of the one who fulfills prophecy, of the one who is prophet, priest, and king. "There is only one mediator between man and God."

I find the writings of Bahaullah, the primary prophet of Baha'i, full of beautiful truths; but when he speaks of Jesus—though he gives him great honor and respect—he does not recognize him as the person Jesus himself claimed to be.

Jesus identified himself in the Scriptures as the Christ, the one perfect sacrifice, God's only Son. Moses does not make a similar claim, nor Mohammad. (Krishna might be said to, but he is in that other set of religions which we'll touch on later in this course.) When Bahaullah claims to be the fulfillment of Jesus Christ, or the return of Jesus Christ, he is contradicting Christ's own promise that he would never leave his people. Just as Jesus stands apart from the other prophets as the fulfillment of prophecy, so Christianity stands apart from the other religions as the fulfilled religion: fulfilled by the constant presence of the living Christ.

Which might lead you to another possibility, the possibility that the great truths Baha'i proclaims are not new truths for the age we live in, but the old truths inherent in God's Word and derived by Bahaullah from his background and commitment to the Islamic traditions. And that without a proper recognition of Christ's redeeming work in delivering his creation from sin and restoring it to true fellowship with God, Baha'i is a beautiful but incomplete competitor, again one of the pale imitators of Christianity.

Reasons I, ©1981, Board of Publications of the Christian Reformed Church, 2850 Kalamazoo Ave. SE, Grand Rapids, MI 49560

Response 2

TRANSCENDENTAL MEDITATION

Jerry's right. Most of us are caught up in lives that are too busy, too noisy, too pressured—like Mike we usually have to leave in twenty minutes. We know we need to "get it all together." And a technique like TM, which promises to help us do just that, sounds very appealing.

But Jerry's information on TM is incomplete. He's glossed over several claims that an alert Christian ought to investigate more clearly.

In his eagerness to "sell" his friends this new system of "self-improvement," Jerry offers scientific evidence that TM is good for your health. It's worth noting that many of these claims arise from tests and surveys conducted by TM practitioners themselves—tests used, seemingly, as a form of advertising. Still the evidence in TM's favor is pretty convincing: meditators *do* seem to gain control over areas of their lives which earlier threatened them and they *do* seem to discover a saner perception of their place in this complex world. So the question is not whether TM works, but whether it is a technique *Christians* should use.

That brings us back to the basic question any Christian should ask himself before deciding to use TM: is it a religion? Jerry claims that the Maharishi has removed the religious aspects of the meditation technique, retaining a method anyone can use, regardless of his or her particular faith. But in saying this, he's ignoring a few things. Regardless of what it calls itself, TM makes some distinctively religious claims: it describes itself as the solution to humanity's most urgent problems, the fundamental healing of humanity's sickness. Also, Jerry is missing the significance of the *puja,* the song the instructor chants during the mantra ceremony. The *puja* clearly connects the offering and meditation with a Hindu tradition that has several implications a Christian ought to consider.

First, Hindus teach that all forms of worship address the same deity; for all is finally one. Christianity, Islam, and Buddhism are all equally acceptable approaches to the Divine Reality, the Brahman or God. Which path makes no difference when all lead to the same goal—only the traveling is important.

Second, the object of Hindu meditation (and therefore TM) is not to reach out toward God but to isolate oneself from that God in an effort to construct a silence in which only the Self remains. To the meditator, Self becomes all-important—Self becomes an expression of God. Obviously, this egocentric meditation runs into direct confrontation with God-centered Christianity.

It's this conflict that Jerry and others involved in TM must be led to see. Christians are not against meditation. In fact, the Bible urges us to meditate. Prayer, Scripture study, and meditation are a rich and deeply developed area within the Christian faith. If Jerry has benefited so much from meditation, he should be encouraged to continue—but as a Christian, not as a Hindu. In the book *Christian Yoga,* a French Catholic mystic clearly defines how a Christian is to proceed if he or she wants to practice Yoga apart from Hindu beliefs and implication. Such a book would be valuable to Jerry and his friends.

Why Christian Yoga but not TM? Transcendental Meditation practices deception by claiming to be a purely secular technique. It is a religion that leads a person towards a silence—a silence in which she listens to a Self divorced from the Lord of creation, the Lord who offered redemption to every lost self through Christ. As such Transcendental Meditation is inconsistent and incompatible with the Christian faith.

The great masters of Yoga never stop asserting and claiming that their practices are independent of all religions, that they will fit any credo. . .[but]. . .their theories and even the principles of Yoga as they expound them are constantly overlaid by leading concepts of a spirituality that is fundamentally Hindu.

Jean Marie Déchanet. *Christian Yoga*, p. 54

Maharishi's teaching feeds on the insatiable spiritual thirst of a race secretly convinced of its divinity but never at ease in it because of all the contrary evidence of man's creaturehood. An "innocent" technique to tap the "unlimited potential" of inner divinity reassures fallen man of his autonomy.

David Haddon, "Transcendental Meditation Challenges the Church," *Christianity Today*, April 9, 1976, p. 19

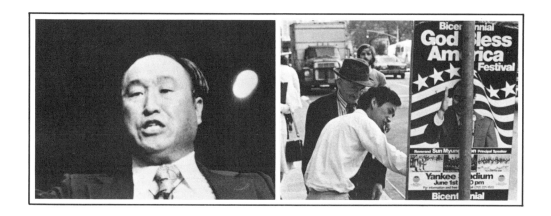

Response 1

THE UNIFICATION CHURCH

Mr. Howard's meeting with Sandy, a young woman who has been profoundly changed by both internal and external experiences, poses questions each of us may face in similar or widely different circumstances. What should he say? What should he do? Before suggesting an approach for Mr. Howard (or for ourselves), let's examine some alternatives that have been tried in the past.

The attempt to *deprogram* a Moonie is perhaps the most dramatic and questionable possibility. Using Mr. Howard's information to locate Sandy, her parents could hire a professional agent who specializes in *deprogramming* persons believed to have been brainwashed into joining a cult such as the Unification Church. A trap may be set, using Benny as bait. And once Sandy is lured into such a meeting, she will be held prisoner. For days or weeks she will be harrassed, literally forced to abandon her "new family" and their beliefs. For months afterwards, parents and friends will keep a close watch. Depending a great deal on Sandy herself, this attempt may succeed or fail, but not without scars.

As another alternative, Mr. Howard might try to continue his theological argument. He could mention several points at which the theology of the Unification Church bluntly contradicts the theology of the historic Christian faith. The Moonies cite Scriptures for their purposes, and Mr. Howard might try citing them for his own.

Or he might bide his time. He might tell himself that there is nothing he can reasonably be expected to do—Sandy is old enough to decide things for herself. Perhaps after a while she'll "come to her senses."

Deprogram, argue theology, or stay out of the whole thing—are these the only options? And if so, are they valid approaches?

We can probably agree that deprogramming may not be the best way to approach the Moonie, though in individual cases it might appear the only way. The most compelling reason for rejecting deprogramming is that it employs the same devices and tactics that parents and others accuse the Moonies of using in their recruitment of new members. One can't easily accuse a group of using unfair methods to compel a new recruit to accept its point of view and then use the same methods to compel the recruit to reject that point of view. Besides, deprogramming can backfire. And when it fails (as it frequently does) it can strengthen the determination of the *victim* to identify more closely with the members of the cult.

Arguing theology is also suspect. It is likely that the convert to the Unification Church has not made his move on the basis of his conviction regarding Moonie beliefs or statements but rather out of a desire to participate in a community where he experiences love and a sense of purpose.

If this is true, the convert has very likely accepted the church's beliefs more out of respect for those in authority than out of conviction born of carefully examining the teachings or beliefs themselves. Thus to argue religion will cause the cult member to withdraw into a defensive position—not to defend the doctrine, but rather the authority of the person behind it. And an absolute commitment to a figure of authority is usually strengthened by the attack of an outsider.

Does this mean Mr. Howard or Sandy's parents should give up and simply wait?

No. They may have to wait, but that waiting should not be simple. They must, while waiting, convey to Sandy how willing they are to accept her at any moment should she reach out to them. They should be developing an understanding of their own faith and that of the Moonies, so that when they do talk together they will be able to discuss doctrine with Sandy without angry confrontation.

And they can examine themselves while they wait. And pray. What did Sandy need that was lacking in her home and church? And why was it lacking? In fairness to Sandy we can only ask her to return to her "first family" when Mr. Howard, and Sandy's parents, and we ourselves have prepared a Christian church and home that is able to meet her deepest needs.

What finally affected me was a Bible passage that Patrick read to me: "Ye shall know the truth and the truth shall make you free." As I started to think, I felt as though a light had been turned on in the room and a burden lifted from my shoulders. I really was free.

Ex-Moonie Cynthia Slaughter, *Time*, June 14, 1976

In a paper examining the theology of the Unification Church, the Commission on Faith and Order of the National Council of the Churches of Christ in the U.S.A. listed four "affirmations" by which one could define "continuity with the Christian faith."
1. *Essential to Christian identity is the biblical affirmation that Jesus of Nazareth is the Christ, the eternal Word of God made flesh.*
2. *The life, death and resurrection of Jesus are the ground and means of the salvation of persons and of the whole creation.*
3. *The triune God—Father, Son and Holy Spirit—has acted as Creator, Redeemer and Sanctifier identifying with the suffering and need of the world and is effectively saving it from sin, death and the powers of evil.*
4. *There is an essential relationship between faith in the saving work of the triune God and obedient response of the believing community.*

The paper goes on to say:
In the light of this definition of continuity with the Christian faith, we conclude:
1. *The Unification Church is not a Christian church.*
   a. *Its doctrine of the nature of the Triune God is erroneous.*
   b. *Its Christology is incompatible with Christian teaching and belief.*
   c. *Its teaching on salvation and the means of grace is inadequate and faulty.*

2. *The claims of the Unification Church to Christian identity cannot be recognized.*
    a. *The role and authority of Scripture are compromised in the teachings of the Unification Church.*
    b. *Revelations are invoked as divine and normative in* Divine Principle *which contradict basic elements of Christian faith.*
    c. *A "new, ultimate, final truth" is presented to complete and supplant all previously recognized religious teachings, including those of Christianity.*

"Occasional Bulletin of Missionary Research," July 1977, p. 23

Reasons I, ©1981, Board of Publications of the Christian Reformed Church, 2850 Kalamazoo Ave. SE, Grand Rapids, MI 49560